C0-DAW-915

Supply Chain Information Technology

WITHDRAWN
UTSA Libraries

Supply Chain Information Technology

David L. Olson

Supply Chain Information Technology

Copyright © Business Expert Press, LLC, 2012.

All rights reserved. No part of this publication may be reproduced, stored in a retrieval system, or transmitted in any form or by any means—electronic, mechanical, photocopy, recording, or any other except for brief quotations, not to exceed 400 words, without the prior permission of the publisher.

First published in 2011 by
Business Expert Press, LLC
222 East 46th Street, New York, NY 10017
www.businessexpertpress.com

ISBN-13: 978-1-60649-360-1 (paperback)
ISBN-13: 978-1-60649-361-8 (e-book)

DOI 10.4128/9781606493618

A publication in the Business Expert Press Supply and Operations Management collection

Collection ISSN: 2156-8189 (print)
Collection ISSN: 2156-8200 (electronic)

Cover design by Jonathan Pennell
Interior design by Scribe Inc.

First edition: January 2012

10 9 8 7 6 5 4 3 2 1

Printed in the United States of America.

Library
University of Texas
at San Antonio

Abstract

The target market for this book is practitioners in the supply chain management field, one of the fastest growing fields in our economy. The rapid growth in computer technology provides supply chain managers with valuable tools to better coordinate and control their operations. This book seeks to describe systems available to give supply chains information system support, demonstrating key tasks with demonstrated analytic techniques.

Keywords

Supply chain management, information systems, information technology, enterprise resource planning systems

Contents

CHAPTER 1

Supply Chain Information Systems

The ability to access global production and services has revolutionized business. Supply chain networks move inventories of various kinds from source to consumption. Being able to work with producers around the world provides opportunities to balance low cost with risk mediation. While logistics usually is associated with moving material, supply chains today can include intangibles such as services as well as inventories of goods. Using the Internet enables linking together supply chain networks in practically any business application, production or services.

Organizations such as Dell and Hewlett-Packard have operated collaborative supply chains with each partner focusing on a few key strategic activities. Supply chains also include organizations such as the military and nonprofit organizations like the Red Cross and Red Crescent. In the retail arena, Walmart has been very successful in the past in linking thousands of sources with their millions of customers. Organizations such as Bank of America have viewed their service operations as key to their success and evaluate their entire service supply chain seeking to apply the same general principles as lean manufacturing, focusing on providing maximum value at minimum overall cost. Information systems are needed to make these supply chains work.

Supply Chain Management

Supply chain management became a common term in the 1980s, heavily influenced by Japanese manufacturing processes such as those developed by Toyota, such as just-in-time (JIT) and lean manufacturing. In the 1990s electronic data interchange (EDI) made it possible to coordinate chains of organizations worldwide. This enabled integration of participant supply chain elements into cooperative components sharing information and enabling coordinated planning, operations, and monitoring of performance. There was a focus on core competencies, abandoning the vertical integration of Standard Oil, U.S. Steel, and Alcoa and replacing it with linkages of independent organizations specializing in what they did best. This encompassed the entire product process to include design, manufacture, distribution, marketing, selling, and service. Agile supply chains such as Motorola and Panasonic are flexible, enabling changing the set of partners for given markets, regions, or channels, accessing the specific price/quality mix that enable organizations to be competitive.

Original equipment manufacturers (OEMs) shifted from making products to become brand owners. These brand owners needed to know what was going on across their entire supply chain, with the need to control from above rather than from within. Standard Oil in 1900 desired to control everything from within, seeking to own all elements in their supply chain. Conversely, Nike doesn't make shoes anymore. They coordinate activities from design to retail through communication supported by a variety of information systems linked across their supply chain.

Supply Chain Processes

Collaboration across supply chains requires integration of all supply chain activities. This requires a continuous flow of information. Key supply chain processes include the following:

- Product development
- Procurement to include outsourcing/partnerships
- Manufacturing
- Physical distribution
- Customer relationship management (CRM)
- Performance measurement

Product development can be obtained by linking customers and suppliers. Customers can express their needs (desires), while the supply chain organization can contribute what is possible. Communication enables identification of a product with a competitive life cycle.

Procurement (sourcing) involves selection of supply chain members. This can be for specific products or services, so that an organization like Walmart might have literally millions of temporary sourcing arrangements. A stable supply chain will have relationships benefiting all parties. Outsourcing refers to procuring sources outside the OEM organization. Outsourcing is broader, however, in that it can refer to obtaining any part of a tangible product or intangible service. Information systems can use EDI and web links to communicate rapidly, enabling effective cost and risk management. Procurement generally involves obtaining materials and components. Outsourcing enables many opportunities to develop a more cost-efficient (or lower risk) supply chain. This comes at the cost of requiring significantly more coordination.

A *manufacturing* process can be developed based on what the OEM organization selects as the best combination of cost and risk over the total product life cycle. Manufacturing processes should be flexible to respond to changes in market conditions. The activities of planning, scheduling, inventory, transportation, and coordination across the supply chain require software coordination.

Physical distribution involves moving products (or services) through the supply chain, ultimately reaching customers. The specific routing is referred to as a channel in marketing and can include a variety of transportation media to move goods. In a service context, the channel can involve the routing of who a customer interacts with to get the service desired.

CRM is the management of the relationships between the providing organization and its customers. Customer service provides information from the customers and has the ability to give customers real-time information on product availability, price, and delivery.

Linking independent elements to work together to deliver goods and/or services is flexible and enables rapid change to comply with new circumstances that are commonly encountered in contemporary business. By expanding beyond the core organization, a need to monitor performance is needed. Some of the key measures of effective supply chain management include cost, service, productivity, use of assets, and quality. This is often implemented through monitoring customer perceptions and identifying best practices as benchmarks to evaluate supply chain performance.

Supply Chain Information Systems

Many software applications are available for each step in the supply chain process. Many vendors specialize in particular steps supporting part of any one of the six elements given earlier. Each supply chain organization will find that they are best served by various combinations of these software products. Furthermore, as technology evolves, new software is developed to serve specific needs as information systems continue to evolve.

A supply chain management stream can be divided into three main streams: product, information, and finances.

- *Product*—Goods moving from sources through manufacturing processes and ultimately on to a customer, to include services such as customer returns.
- *Information*—Transmitting orders and updating delivery status.
- *Finances*—Credit terms, payment schedules, shipment, and contractual relationships.

Because of advances in manufacturing and distribution systems, the cost of developing new products and services is dropping and time to market is decreasing. This has resulted in increasing demand, local and global competition, and strain on supply chains. Supply chain management (SCM) software links suppliers to databases that show forecasts, current inventory, shipping, or logistics time frames within the customer organization. By giving this access to suppliers, they can better meet their customers' demands. For example, the suppliers can adjust shipping to make certain that their customers have the inventory necessary to meet their customers' needs. They also can monitor unexpected supply chain disruptions to organize alternative routing. Suppliers can download forecasts into their own manufacturing systems to automate their internal processes as well.

Planning applications and execution applications are the two primary types of SCM software:

- *Planning applications* are capable of generating improved plans through use of mathematical algorithms
- *Execution applications* enable tracing goods, managing materials, and exchanging financial information

A number of supply chain systems have evolved over the decades. The first was materials requirements planning (MRP). This was extended to include planning schedules (often labeled MRP-II). Enterprise requirements planning (ERP) systems seek to integrate all organizational information systems, although of course companies will always have special needs outside of an ERP. Nonetheless, ERP systems support much of supply chain activity, to include financial transactions with sources and customers, inventory dealings with sources, forecasting to support planning, MRP to support assembly operations, and many other activities. The trend is for many functions that used to be outside the ERP to be offered as modules within ERP. One case in point is advanced planning system software (APS). There also have been systems marketed as warehouse management systems, transportation management systems, manufacturing execution systems, and the more general logistics management systems, targeted for specific industries such as the military and/or construction. The 21st century has seen a continued expansion of ERP systems to include additional functionality, such as customer relationship management (CRM) and SCM systems as part of the enterprise information system (EIS). There also are other uses of information technology available to support supply chains, such as online marketplaces.

Materials Requirements Planning (MRP)

The term "MRP" is used as a general term to include all MRP versions, namely, MRP-I (i.e., materials requirements planning), Closed-loop MRP (i.e., MRP-I with capacity planning and shop floor management), and MRP-II (i.e., Closed-loop MRP integrated with the other functions such as finance and marketing).[1] The concept of an integrated information system took shape on the factory floor. Manufacturing software developed during the 1960s and 1970s, evolving from simple inventory tracking systems to materials requirements planning (MRP) software. MRP at its core is a time-phased order release system that schedules and releases manufacturing work orders and purchase orders, so that subassemblies and components are available at the assembly station when they are required. Some of the benefits of MRP are reduction of inventories, improved customer service, and enhanced efficiency and effectiveness. MRP software allows a plant manager to plan production and raw materials requirements by working backward from the sales forecast, the prediction of future sales. Thus, the manager first looks at marketing and sales forecasts of demand (what the customer wants), the production schedule needed to meet that demand, calculates the raw materials needed to meet production, and projects raw materials purchase orders to suppliers. For a company with many products, raw materials, and shared production resources, this kind of projection was impossible without a computer to keep track of various inputs.

Electronic data interchange (EDI), the direct computer-to-computer exchange of standard business documents, allowed companies to handle the purchasing process electronically, avoiding the cost and delays resulting from paper purchase order and invoice systems. SCM began with the sharing of long-range production schedules between manufacturers and their suppliers.

The MRP system should provide four basic items of information: when to place the order, how much to order, who to order from, and when the items need to be on hand. MRP systems are used to acquire or fabricate component quantities on time both for internal purposes and for sales and distribution. MRP is a planning instrument geared exclusively to assembly operations. Each manufacturing unit informs its suppliers what parts it needs and when it requires them. The main aim for evolution of MRP was to tackle the problem of "dependent demand," that is, determining how many of a particular component is required knowing the number of finished products.

The next stage of MRP-II evolution was just-in-time (JIT) methodology in the late 1980s. MRP-II (manufacturing resource planning) is a method to plan all resources for a manufacturer. A variety of business functions are tied into MRP-II systems, including order processing as in MRP, business planning, sales and operations planning, production planning, master production scheduling, capacity requirements planning, and capacity planning. MRP-II systems are integrated with accounting and finance subsystems to produce reports including business plans, shipping budgets, inventory projections, and purchase plans. A major purpose of MRP-II is to integrate primary functions (i.e., production, marketing, and finance) and other functions such as personnel, engineering, and purchasing into the planning process to improve the efficiency of the manufacturing enterprise.

Many within the operations management field consider ERP as a natural extension of MRP-II. The APICS Association for Operations Management definition for ERP is a method for effective planning and control of all resources needed to take, make, ship, and account for customer orders.[2] There is at least some truth to this view, but ERP systems are even more comprehensive than simply on manufacturing operations. ERP systems are found in practically all types of large organizations, including chemical facilities and even universities. MRP-II functions are covered by production planning and other ERP modules.

Advanced Planning Systems (APSs)

Computer technology makes it possible for improvements at both the cost and value ends of the supply chain. Demand uncertainties can be better managed through improved inventory demand forecasting, reduction of inventories, and improved transportation costs through optimization of coordinated activities across the supply chain. Advanced planning systems (APSs) provide decision support by using operational data to analyze material flows throughout the supply chain. This supports the business functions of purchasing, production, and distribution and through the entire spectrum of planning. Purchasing is supported by planning and MRP. Production is supported by strategic, master, and production planning as well as short-term scheduling. Distribution is supported by distribution planning and transportation planning. These planning systems interact, enabling management of demand across the supply chain. APS products are shown in Table 1.1.

Table 1.1. APS Software Suppliers[3]

i2	Consulting and managed services
Manugistics	Resource planning and supply chain management
Wassermann	Smart manufacturing, distribution and after-sales services, procurement management, and information technology
Visopt	Supply chain optimization for process industries
Logic-tools	Supply chain optimization tools to complement existing software
Fygir	Optimized scheduling and planning
Quintig	Suite of supply chain planning tools
Seeburger	Business integration platform
Infor	ERP with APS module option
proAlpha	Multiresource, real-time supply chain optimization
Axxom	Mobile supply chain optimization and planning
Epicor	Acquired Vista and Vantage—ERP with APS module option
Oracle	11i advanced planning and scheduling system
SAP	SAP APO

Source. Extracted from company websites.

Advanced planning systems use historical demand data as the basis of forecasts that are used to manage future demand. However, in order to optimize systems, a certain level of stability is required. John D. Rockefeller was able to manipulate demand for petroleum products over 100 years ago, obtaining the stability he needed. Demand manipulation is still possible in some markets today but is much more difficult. The idea of supply chain optimization is more difficult to implement in conditions of constant product innovation, highly volatile global demand, and increased product customization (such as applied by Dell and other computer vendors allowing customers to custom design their computer systems online). This turbulent market environment makes it difficult to obtain extensive pertinent demand history. It is easy to collect data, but demand changes too rapidly to take advantage of it for extended periods of time.

Warehouse Management Systems (WMSs)

Warehouse management systems provide the functionality of tracking parts throughout a supply chain. Systems such as HighJump Software and RedPrairie Corp offer products using electronic input such as bar code scanning to track materiel through the supply chain system, maintaining accurate information flow to parallel physical flow. Radio-frequency identification (RFID) technology provides another form of electronic data input to WMSs.

Manufacturing Execution Systems (MESs)

Manufacturing execution systems appeared in the mid-1990s, evolving as all other supply chain information technology. The original focus was to manage demand on manufacturing organizations with respect to quality, standards, cost reduction, schedule, and ability to react to change. With time, functions have emphasized support traceability. MES functionality now integrates support to most manufacturing execution processes from release of production orders to finished goods delivery. MES also triggers supply chain replenishment upstream (telling sources that replenishment inventory is needed). These systems use a common user interface and data system to integrate support to multiple locations or organizations within a supply chain. An MES offers the following functionality:

- Scheduling
- Process management
- Document control
- Data collection/acquisition
- Labor management
- Quality management
- Production unit dispatch
- Maintenance management
- Product tracking
- Performance analysis
- Resource allocation and tracking

An MES can interact between the organizational ERP and the shop floor, taking production orders from the ERP and allocating machines and labor to tasks or products. Real status from the shop floor in turn is passed on to the ERP to update resource availability, track products and inventory, and record production. Logistics functions in the ERP include plant production scheduling, shipping, and inventory. The MES will translate that to execution in the form of dispatching, detailed production scheduling, and tracking materiel.

Transportation Management Systems (TMSs)

Transportation management systems provide software support at an affordable level to control shipping. A variety of alternative sources are available to increase visibility and generate more efficient solutions to move materiel in an increasingly complex environment involving many risks (piracy, war, regulations). Functionality provided includes transportation mode planning, optimization models, and workflow management.[4]

TMS software can be obtained from vendors, some of whom are listed here:[5]

- Accuship
- GEOCOMtms
- HighJump (acquired Pinnacle)
- Infor
- i2 Technologies

- JDA (acquired Manugistics)
- Pitney Bowes
- Oracle (acquired G-Log)
- QAD (acquired Precision Software)
- RedPrairie
- SAP
- Sterling Commerce (acquired Nistevo)
- UPS Logistics Technologies

This list includes the two flagship ERP vendors: Oracle and SAP. It also demonstrates the volatility of the industry, showing a number of acquisitions. Other means of TMS acquisition include in-house development, hosting by an ASP, or software as a service. Firms also have options with respect to software within specific branches of the organization, or enterprise-wide support.

ERP

In the early 1970s, business computing relied on centralized mainframe computer systems. Today it is reported that 80% of Fortune 500 firms use ERP systems to manage operations.[6] These systems proved their value by providing a systematic way to measure what businesses did financially. The reports these systems delivered could be used for analysis of variance with budgets and plans, and served as a place to archive business data. Computing provided a way to keep records much more accurately, and on a massively larger scale than was possible through manual means. But from our perspective at the beginning of the 21st century, that level of computer support was primitive.

Business computing systems were initially applied to those functions that were easiest to automate and that called for the greatest levels of consistency and accuracy. Payroll and accounting functions were an obvious initial application. Computers can be programmed to generate accurate paychecks, considering tax and overtime regulations of any degree of complexity. They also can implement accounting systems for tax, cost, and other purposes because these functional applications tend to have precise rules that cover almost every case, so that computers can be entrusted to automatically and rapidly take care of everything related to these functions.

Prior to 2000, ERP systems catered to very large firms, who could afford the rather high costs of purchasing ERP systems. Even focusing on a selected few modules would typically cost firms $5 million and up for software. After 2000, demand dropped, in part because firms were often concerned with Y2K issues prior to 2000, which motivated many ERP system acquisitions. Demand noticeably dropped off after 2000 came and went. Vendors reacted in a number of ways. First, the market consolidated, with Oracle purchasing PeopleSoft (who had earlier acquired JD Edwards). Microsoft acquired a number of smaller ERP software products, consolidating them into Microsoft Dynamics, which caters to a smaller-priced market, thus serving a needed gap in ERP coverage for small businesses. Notably, SAP advertises that they can serve small business too. But it appears that they are more valuable in the large-scale enterprise market. Additionally, there are many other systems to include open-sourced ERP systems (at least for acquisition) like Compiere in France. Many countries, such as China, India, and others have thriving markets for ERP systems designed specifically for local conditions, although SAP and Oracle have customers all over the globe.

An enterprise information system (EIS) is appearing as a term for the addition of what used to be independent add-on software such as supply chain management (SCM) systems and customer relationship management (CRM) to the core ERP. This trend manifested itself initially when Oracle purchased Siebel Systems, the leading CRM provider. SAP responded by acquiring their own CRM, and both vendors have added SCM functionality within their systems as well. The difference between ERP and EIS is primarily marketing semantics, so we will use ERP for both older and newer versions. One trend among ERP vendors is to expand their functionality to provide services formerly supplied by supply chain vendors such as Manugistics and i2 Technologies.[7] SAP has introduced mySAP.com, which is an open collaborative system integrating SAP and non-SAP software. SAP APO supports supply chain activities such as forecasting, scheduling, and other logistics-related activities. PeopleSoft has Enterprise Performance Management to support decisions at many levels. JD Edwards products have support for planning and execution. Oracle's 11i advanced planning and scheduling system was designed to automate customer, supplier, and firm interactions. Vendors are moving toward greater integration of supply chain products.

The ERP concept is not applied merely for the manufacturing environment but for all kinds of enterprises. Early ERP systems focused on manufacturing, although they quickly expanded to support all sorts of organizations. ERP facilitates enterprise-wide integrated information systems covering all functional areas and performs core corporate activities and enlarges customer service. ERP is a business management system that seeks to combine all aspects of the organization. It is capable of taking care of planning, manufacturing, sales, and marketing. The concept is to integrate legacy systems within a coordinated integrated system. Typically, an ERP system uses database systems, which are integrated with each other.

Common ERP Features: An ERP system is not merely the integration of diverse enterprise processes mentioned earlier but also can possess key characteristics to meet the requirements. Features often found in an ERP include the following:

- *Best business practices*—Incorporation of processes evaluated as the best in the world
- *Comprehensive*—Integrating as many business computing functions as possible, with a single database
- *Modular*—An open system architecture allowing incorporation of those modules needed for the organization
- *Flexible*—Capable of response to changing enterprise needs, to include Open DataBase Connectivity (ODBC)
- *External linkage*—Capable of linking external organizations, especially within supply chains

Among the many reasons to adopt an ERP, they offer an integrated system shared by all users rather than a diverse set of computer applications, which rarely can communicate with each other, and with each having its own set of data and files. ERP provides a means to coordinate information system assets and information flows across the organization. The main benefit is the elimination of suborganizational silos that focus on their own problems rather than serving the interests of the overall organization. On the downside, ERP systems impose one procedure for the entire organization, which requires everyone to conform to the new system. ERP systems are thus less flexible. But the benefits of integration are usually much greater than the costs of conformity.

Data can be entered once, at the most accurate source, so that all users share the same data. This can be very beneficial, because shared data is used more and by more people, which leads to much more complete and accurate data. As errors are encountered, users demand corrections, but this is limited because a set of procedures is needed to ensure that changes do not introduce new errors. This makes it harder to make corrections, but again, this added inconvenience is usually well worth the gains of data integration.

ERP systems also can provide better ways of doing things. This idea is the essence of best practices, a key SAP system component. The downside to best practices is that they take a great deal of effort in identifying the best way to proceed with specific business functions, and that they often can involve significant change in how organizational members do their work. Further, as with any theory, what is considered best by one is often not considered best by all.

ERP systems are usually adopted with the expectation that they are going to yield lower computing costs in the long run. Ideally, adopting one common way of doing things is simpler and involves less effort to provide computing support to an organization. In practice, savings are often not realized, due to failure to anticipate all the detailed nuances of user needs, as well as the inevitable changes in the business environment that call for different best practices and computer system relationships. Training needs are typically underbudgeted in ERP projects. Furthermore, these training budgets don't usually include the hidden costs of lost productivity as employees cope with complex new systems. Table 1.2 recaps these pros and cons of ERP systems.

Table 1.2. ERP Pros and Cons[8]

Factor	Pro	Con
System integration	Improved understanding across users	Less flexibility
Data integration	Greater accuracy	Harder to make corrections
Best practices	More efficient methods	Imposition of how people do their work Less freedom and creativity
Cost of computing	More efficient system planned	Changing needs Underbudgeted training expense Hidden costs of implementation

The key rationales for implementing ERP systems are the following:

- *Technology*—More powerful, integrated computer systems with greater flexibility and lower IT cost
- *Business practices*—Implementation of better ways of accomplishing tasks yielding better operational quality and greater productivity
- *Strategy*—Cost advantages can be gained through more efficient systems leading to improved decision making, more business growth, and better external linkages
- *Competitive advantage*—If an organization's competitors adopt ERP and gain cost efficiencies as well as serve customers better, organizations will be left with declining clientele, competitive advantage will also arise from providing better customer service

The motivations for ERP adoption were examined by three studies using the same format. Mabert et al. (2000) surveyed over 400 Midwestern U.S. manufacturing organizations about ERP adoption. Olhager and Selldin (2003) replicated that study with 190 manufacturing firms in Sweden. Katerattanakul et al. (2006) again replicated the survey, this time in Korea. These studies reported the following ratings with respect to motivation for implementing ERP (see Table 1.3).

Table 1.3. Reasons for Implementing ERP[9]

Reason	United States	Sweden	Korea
Replace legacy systems	4.06	4.11	3.42
Simplify and standardize systems	3.85	3.67	3.88
Improve interactions with suppliers and customers	3.55	3.16	3.45
Gain strategic advantage	3.46	3.18	3.63
Link to global activities	3.17	2.85	3.54
Solve the Y2K problem	3.08	2.48	NA
Pressure to keep up with competitors	2.99	2.48	2.94
Ease of upgrading systems	2.91	2.96	3.55
Restructure organization	2.58	2.70	3.33

Rating scale from 1 (not important) to 5 (very important).

Source: Extracted from Mabert et al. (2000), Olhager and Selldin (2003), Katerattanakul et al. (2006).

Initially, fear of Y2K was a major concern. The Swedish survey was later than the one in the United States, and that might explain the lower rating for this item in the Swedish study. The later Korean study did not ask about this dated issue. The U.S. response was actually neutral (only slightly higher than 3), but Y2K clearly was a factor in ERP adoption in the mid- to late-1990s. However, more important reasons were always present. In the first two studies, replacing legacy systems received a high positive response. The desire to simplify and standardize systems had the second highest rating in the first two studies and had the highest rating in the later Korean study.

There were two other reasons that received relatively high ratings in the United States (a bit lower in Sweden). These were to improve interactions with suppliers and customers, which is one way to gain strategic advantage. The supply chain aspects of ERP have led vendors to modify their products to be more open, although work continues to be needed in this direction (and seems to be proceeding). Linking to global activities was slightly positive in the U.S. survey, more negative in the Swedish study, and relatively higher in the Korean study.

Three other potential reasons received low ratings in both studies. Pressure to keep up with competitors received neutral support in the U.S. study. Ease of upgrading systems is a technical reason that received neutral support both in the United States and in Sweden. Restructuring the organization was rated lower.

From these studies, we infer that ERP systems are an important means to upgrade the quality of information systems. They can provide organizations with coordinated systems that have higher-quality data. Once the kinks are worked out, this information may be available in a more responsive way. Not all evidence indicates lower costs, but most evidence does indicate higher-quality information systems.

ERP and SCM: Originally ERP tools were not considered for SCM and thus the information flow between various members of the supply chain was slow. This was because until the late 1990s the concentration of organizations was on improving the internal efficiency alone. Organizations however, soon realized that although internal efficiency is important, its benefit would be limited unless complemented by increased efficiency across the supply chain. They also realized that, accurate flow of real-time information across the supply chain was the key to success in the emerging business climate, which was characterized by rapid advances in technology, shorter product life cycles, and so forth. Therefore, organizations started integrating ERP applications with SCM software. This ensures that efficiency was achieved across the supply chain, including a seamless flow of information. ERP became a vital link in the integrated supply chain as it serves as the integrated planning and control system.

In summary, ERP applications help in effectively delivering SCM in the following ways:

- *Data sharing*—They can create opportunities to share data across supply chain members, which can help managers in making better decisions. They also make available wider scope to supply chain managers by providing access to much broader information.
- *Real-time information*—ERP systems can provide real-time information, which can be great help in supply chain decisions. For example, ordering raw materials can be based on the inventory details provided by the ERP systems.

Web-based technologies have revolutionized the way business is conducted, and supply chain management and ERP are no exceptions. In order to leverage the benefits offered by this new technology enabler, ERP systems are being "web-enabled." The Internet allows linking websites to back-end systems like ERP and providing connections to host of external parties. The benefits of such a system are that customers have direct access to the supplier's ERP system and that the vendors in turn can provide real-time information about inventory, pricing, order, and shipping status. The Internet thus provides an interface between the ERP system and the supply chain members allowing real-time flow of reliable and consistent information. To illustrate a benefit of web-enabling ERP, such a facility allows customers to go online and configure their own products and get price information and immediately gets to know whether the configured product is in stock or not. This is made possible because the customer's request directly accesses the ERP system of the supplier.

Online Marketplaces

Online marketplaces (OLMs) are exchange mechanisms that can benefit suppliers and purchasers by providing a more competitive environment with broader access. E-marketplaces aggregate buyers, sellers, content, and business services. They also provide a single point of integration for interaction of buyers and sellers. A buyer can log on to an e-marketplace, issue a request for proposal, and be flooded with bids. This creates a problem of bid comparison and interpretation. OLMs also provide services to help sift through large numbers of bids. Different types of OLMs are given in Table 1.4, demonstrating different transaction methods.

Auction-based OLMs are commonly used. One use of auction-based OLMs is as an exchange, seeking simultaneous bids and offers to determine efficient prices. Future contract variants allow buyers to lock in supplies or hedge prices. Pure auctions seek only bids to establish prices for unique products. Reverse auctions do the same, only from the perspective of offers rather than bids. Metacatalogs focus on reducing search costs rather than on pricing. Mall-based OLMs allow buyers to surf a single site, with visits to individual areas representing different suppliers.

Table 1.4. Types of Online Marketplace Methods

Transaction method	
Auction-based	Exchange seeking simultaneous bids
Future contract variants	For risk reduction
Pure auction systems	To establish prices for buyers
Reverse auctions	To establish prices for sellers
Metacatalogs	Reduce search costs
Mall-based	Access multiple suppliers at single site

Example Application of a Supply Chain Management System

Investment in information technology has become the single largest capital expense for U.S. firms, accounting for up to 50% of all capital investment. Zong Dai presented a case study of the implementation of an ERP system at the corporate level with the intent of demonstrating the relationship of business processes with ERP, and how ERP systems can provide sustainable competitive advantage in supply chain operations. Wyeth, a global pharmaceutical research and manufacturing company, was studied through site visits, interviews, and examination of documents such as annual reports, archived records, and electronic databases. Wyeth develops and markets pharmaceuticals, vaccines, and biotechnology products for both human and animal health care.

In 1994 Wyeth divested a number of assets that were not related to their chosen strategic focus on human and animal health care. At that time Wyeth's processes were accomplished through a paper-driven process. They acquired companies that contributed to this selected strategy. As part of their new strategy, Wyeth wanted to develop effective information technology. Their business initiatives were to transform business processes and systems into a globally integrated supply chain, restructuring product lines to reduce indirect goods and services and improve system interoperability. An SAP ERP system was selected with the intent of implementation by 2000 as a means to upgrade Wyeth's MRP system to implement data warehousing. A component of the system was SAP's Advanced Planner and Optimizer (APO), software applications to support supply chain management activities through improving production planning, pricing, scheduling, and product shipping.

The system implementation was accomplished by an internal team of three Wyeth IT professionals working with three SAP consultants. The greatest challenges proved to be business process reengineering. The entire process from sourcing to receipt of payment from customers was to be electronically automated and stored in one central database. The purchasing process was streamlined through business process reengineering (BPR) to enable the most cost-effective procurement.

The system also kept information on orders, receipts, and inventory balances current and available in real time. When the planning module generates production needs, vendor selections are automatically made considering lead times to ensure uninterrupted production. Pricing, availability checks, product comparisons, and vendor selection are instantly available. Orders are immediately printed and distributed by the system, with electronic verification of invoices to ensure automatic payment to vendors when goods are received.

The greatest challenge encountered was process and change management. Training Wyeth personnel was challenging but was successfully accomplished through multiple methods. These methods included instructor lectures, web tutorials, and other training media.

Wyeth was able to utilize their SAP system to consolidate business processes across its supply chain. The system was credited with improving Wyeth financial performance.

Source: Adapted from Zong Dai (2008).

Conclusion

In the past, vertical integration was a way to gain efficiency in supply chains. Today, vertical integration doesn't work as well, because specialty organizations have developed to perform specific tasks very efficiently. Efficiency is gained today through supply chains linking specialists throughout the vertical business hierarchy.

A number of software systems are available to support supply chains. This chapter reviewed MRP, APS, and ERP. OLM software was briefly described as an example of other software support. ERP systems were initially focused on integrating internal operations. Their high investment cost and often rigid procedures made them barriers to effective supply chain linkage. However, recent trends show movement toward more open systems that allow closer coordination across supply chains. One way to accomplish this efficiency would be through all elements in a supply chain adopting the same ERP vendor products, as well as software enhancements. However, this is not economically viable for most supply chain components. Many suppliers may not have the millions necessary to invest in technology adopted by the core company in the supply chain.

Other approaches are toward open ERP software. Advanced Planning Systems were originally developed to enhance the ability of firms to deal with other organizations in their supply chain. More recently, the trend among ERP vendors is to provide this functionality within their products, especially through Internet technology. Lean manufacturing is another philosophy related to gaining efficiency in production operations. While the concepts of lean manufacturing initially seem in conflict with the idea of ERP, there have been imaginative developments allowing ERP systems to support lean manufacturing.

ERP deployment, management, and evolution are significant operational concerns in today's cost-conscious business climate. The performance of enterprise applications designed to streamline ERP processes and operations is dependent on the fundamental network infrastructure. Companies should take a holistic view of their mission critical applications and networking environments and include best-in-class networking solutions.

Enterprises have long made flamboyant statements about getting closer to their customers and streamlining operations. ERP, CRM, and SCM applications and the organizations implementing them are in part, "bringing teeth" to those superior intentions. It is not a trouble-free process, however. In reality, the highly publicized failures of these initiatives have in some minds brought concern about these applications and their possible benefits. However, more and more organizations are moving ahead with these initiatives, and the successful organizations will gain from higher margins, better customer relations, and improved back office operations.

The core idea of ERP is complete integration of an organization's computing system. Despite obvious advantages to vendors of each adopting organization installing the entire suite of modules offered, however, only about half of the implementations seem to be of this nature. It is very common for organizations to select modules, which makes great sense because not every organization needs every module vendors develop. In fact, vendors seem to recognize this through their recent emphasis on products tailored to specific industry.

Organizations may have other very important reasons to implement ERP products differently than the vendors' design. A very important one is that full system implementation is very expensive. By selecting particular modules, organizations can cut initial implementation costs significantly. While vendors might argue that in the long run this might be more ineffective than full implementation now, in practice information systems projects rarely go as planned, nor do they tend to stay within originally planned budgets. Thus, organizations reduce risk greatly by trying particular modules first, often seeing how the new system is digested by the organization, before plunging to additional modules.

There also is a difference in the difficulty of implementing different modules. Financial and accounting modules are typically installed first, as they involve the most structured application. This makes it easier to implement, and easier for the organization to digest. Other modules such as materials management and planning also tend to work well. Conversely, support to less structured environments, such as sales and marketing, tend to be more problematic.

Outline of the Book

This chapter introduced various information systems available to support supply chain operations. The second chapter will more completely describe the key supply chain process of MRP and describe its relationship to ERP systems. Chapter 3 will expand discussion of ERP options, to include APS as an available module or as a stand-alone system. Chapter 4 will discuss the relationship of business process reengineering with these integrated systems. Chapter 5 will present a systematic selection technique. Chapter 6 will discuss issues in implementing such systems, along with demonstration of project management in the supply chain software context. Chapter 7 will conclude the book, discussing three issues in implementing these systems.

CHAPTER 2

Development of ERP and SCM

Effective supply chain operations require efficient collaboration across supply chain elements (distributors, manufacturers, suppliers) through sharing key information for coordination. This is usually accomplished through software tools, such as advanced planning systems or linked enterprise resource planning systems (ERPs). Walmart has been very effective in operating at a global level by requiring sources to have SAP systems to link to their ERPs.[1] Dell has developed a profitable supply chain niche in the computer field, not by making computers, but rather through using a made-to-order e-business, relying on a global supply chain for the parts they assemble.[2] They are only two of many supply chain organizations that have prospered through reengineering operations enabling to successfully compete. Supply chains don't have to be private organizations. The U.S. Department of Defense uses software to coordinate logistics for its activities. Even nonprofit organizations like the Red Cross coordinate their supply chains with software support.

As we stated in chapter 1, supply chain management systems began with materials requirements planning (MRP). These systems provided a rational way for assembly manufacturers to control their inventories. This was extended in the 1980s to what was labeled MRP-II. Parallel to that, SAP developed their ERP system, centered on accounting and financial functions. SAP continues to conduct extensive research on best practices for standard business functions and incorporates the knowledge gained into their evolving ERP product. ERP was especially attractive to manufacturing firms, and MRP inventory management and shop-floor scheduling and planning were early functions supported by SAP's ERP systems. In the last decade, more effective advanced planning systems (APSs) have evolved to enable better decision support and control of materials flows, often in conjunction with ERP systems.

ERP Modules

ERP systems in concept cover all computing for an organization. The idea is to centralize data and computation, so that data can be entered once in a clean form and then be used by everyone in the organization (even by supply chain partners outside the organization) with the confidence that the data are correct. However, in practice, ERP vendors sold their software in modules. Modules allow clients to save money by reducing the number of components licensed, focusing on the most important functions first. ERP vendors have recently focused on offering systems tailored to specific clients, such as aerospace, insurance, or medical operations. Table 2.1 gives a list of SAP modules around 2000 (extracted from Brady et al.[3]). Other

Table 2.1. Modules

SAP	Description	Oracle
SD	Sales and distribution: records sales orders and scheduled deliveries, customer information	Marketing Sales Supply chain
MM	Materials management: purchasing and raw materials inventory, work-in-process (WIP), finished goods	Procurement
PP	Production planning: production planning and scheduling, actual production	Manufacturing
QM	Quality management: product inspections, material certifications, quality control	
PM	Plant maintenance: preventive maintenance, resource management	Service
HR	Human resources: recruiting, hiring, training, payroll, benefits	Human resources
FI	Financial accounting: general ledger account transactions, generates financial statements	Financials
CO	Controlling: internal management, cost analysis by cost center	
AM	Asset management: fixed-asset purchase and depreciation	Asset management
PS	Project system: R&D, construction, marketing projects, SAP R/3 implementation	Projects
WF	Workflow: automated R/3, task-flow analysis, prompt actions	Contracts
IS	Industry solutions: best practices	

Sources: Vendor websites, 2005.

vendors have parallel sets of modules, as demonstrated in Table 2.2. This information was extracted from vendor websites like www.oracle.com. As with any current website, content is subject to change.

Module MM covers the functions of MRP. MRP began as an inventory reordering tool in operations involving dependent demand (the demand for materials that are necessary to create the final product). The capability of MRP systems evolved to support planning of all company resources and currently can support business planning, production planning, purchasing, inventory control, shop floor control, cost management, capacity planning, and logistics management. The use of MRP resulted in better inventory and raw materials control, reduced need for clerical support, and reduced lead times in obtaining materials. Improved communication and better integration of planning were also gained.

Relative Module Use

Business computing systems were initially applied to those functions that were easiest to automate and that called for the greatest levels of consistency and accuracy. Payroll and accounting functions were an obvious initial application. Computers can be programmed to generate accurate paychecks, considering tax and overtime regulations of any degree of complexity. They also can implement accounting systems for tax, cost, and other purposes because these functional applications tend to have precise rules that cover almost every case, so that computers can be entrusted to automatically and rapidly take care of everything related to these functions.

The degree of module use was reported by Mabert et al. (2000) and replicated by Olhager and Selldin (2003).[4] Mabert et al. surveyed 479 ERP users from the American Inventory and Inventory Control Society in the Midwestern U.S. in the 1990s. Olhager and Selldin patterned their study after Mabert et al., using 190 Swedish manufacturing firms. Table 2.2 presents information extracted from that study. Those proportions over 90% and under 50% are italicized for emphasis.

The most popular module in the United States was financial and accounting, which is the most obvious application needed by an organization. The Swedish study indicated that materials management, production planning, order entry, and purchasing modules were just as popular. Other modules, given at the bottom of Table 2.2 and each with adoption rates less than 50%, either are not considered as critical or involve less specificity in best practices. These are similar for both studies, although human resources modules were slightly more popular in Sweden. There have been noted differences in the ease in which different modules are implemented. All financial modules tend to be relatively easy to implement. Those modules relating to manufacturing and human resources also have been implemented with notable success. On the other hand, modules supporting less-structured activities, such as sales and marketing, have encountered notable implementation difficulty. Therefore, one reason to implement ERP in modules is because of the relative need for components of the overall system.

Another (and probably the compelling) reason is cost. Full ERP systems cost a reported $5 million for very small versions to over $100 million for very large implementations. The fewer modules implemented, the lower the cost. Additionally, it sometimes makes sense to implement the system in bits (phased implementation) rather than try to bring the entire massive system online at one time (Big Bang implementation). Thus, rolling out an ERP by module sometimes makes sense as well. For a number of reasons, ERP in practice is usually implemented by module.

Table 2.2. Relative ERP Module Use

Module	Use—Midwestern U.S.	Use—Sweden
Financial and accounting	91.5%	87.3%
Materials management	89.2%	91.8%
Production planning	88.5%	90.5%
Order entry	87.7%	92.4%
Purchasing	86.9%	93.0%
Financial control	81.5%	82.3%
Distribution/logistics	75.4%	84.8%
Asset management	57.7%	63.3%
Quality management	44.6%	47.5%
Personnel/human resources	44.6%	57.6%
Maintenance	40.8%	44.3%
R&D management	30.8%	34.2%

Sources: Based on Mabert et al. (2000); Olhager and Selldin (2003).

Variants in Types of ERP Systems

Often firms will apply the concept of *best-of-breed*, mixing modules from different vendors. The Mabert et al. study found that a single ERP package was utilized as the vendor designed in only 40% (56% in Sweden) of the over 400 respondents to their survey. The most common strategic approach in the United States (50%, as opposed to 30% in Sweden) was to supplement a single ERP package. In fewer cases, the idea of best-of-breed was applied (4% in both studies). As might be expected by the enormity of the undertaking, few of the surveyed implementations were entirely constructed in-house (less than 1% in the United States, 2% in Sweden).

The idea of best-of-breed approaches is to take advantage of what is perceived as specific vendor relative advantage in particular areas of application. One vendor's human resource module might be used, in conjunction with another vendor's financial and accounting system, and yet a third vendor's materials management modules. In 1999, Honeywell and AlliedSignal were merged, and the best approaches of each firm's existing ERP systems were examined, with those components judged to be superior retained in the merged firm.[5] Quite often third-party software designed to integrate software applications from several vendors (*middleware*) is needed. The role of middleware products is to enable cross-platform operating system communications. This means that software applications such as e-commerce, data warehouses, customer relationship management, supply chain software, and other enhancements can be added to ERP systems. Middleware also allows connection of best-of-breed modules to the ERP backbone.

If a firm chooses to utilize their own methods within an ERP, Davenport gave the choice between rewriting the code internally or using the existing system with interfaces.[6] Both approaches add time and cost to implementation and thus would dilute the integration benefits of the ERP. The more customization made to an ERP, the less ability to communicate seamlessly within system components and across supplier and customer systems. However, the trade-off is that much less change in employee work processes is necessary. Thus customization reduces the hidden costs of learning the new system by employees (the human side), while increasing the burden on the IT staff. Not customizing makes it much easier on the IT staff but makes employees work much harder to adapt their work to the new system.

Another important concept is the idea of *federalization*. Davenport used this term to describe the process of rolling out different versions of an ERP system in each regional unit, tailoring each location's system to accommodate local operating practices.[7] Hewlett-Packard, Monsanto, and Nestlé have all used this approach, establishing a common core of ERP modules shared by all units but allowing other modules to be operated and controlled locally.

Because of its focus on a key function of supply chain management, we will describe the basic MRP process in greater detail. (Specific commercial software may differ in details.)

Materials Requirements Planning

The MRP system begins with three documents. A forecast for end-items being assembled is needed by time period. A bill of materials (BOM) describes the components that go into an assembled product. It lists each part in a hierarchical tree, by quantities required for each sub-assembly, all the way up to the final end-item. Finally, inventory records describing quantities of each component on hand is needed, as well as managerially determined ordering policies with vendors and lead times.

We use a small example to demonstrate the basic workings of MRP, one of the most important supply chain management processes. MRP begins with a master production schedule showing the requirements for output from the manufacturing facility by time unit (Table 2.3). A second component of the system is inventory and purchasing information, which shows the initial quantity on hand by item, order conditions, lead times, and currently open orders (Table 2.4). Additional inventory information such as safety stocks could also be included. BOMs show the hierarchy of components required to manufacture each end-item and subcomponent (Figures 2.1 through 2.4).

Assume an automobile company produces four types of automobiles. They use a rolling 20-day planning horizon.

Table 2.3. Master Production Schedule

Day	1	2	3	4	5	6	7	8	9	10	11	12	13	14	15	16	17	18	19	20
Sedans	40	30	30	30	25	25	25	25	20	20	20	15	20	15	15	10	10	10	10	10
Roadsters	15	18	17	13	15	16	14	14	13	13	11	9	10	9	8	7	6	6	6	5
Town cars	10	10	10	10	10	10	10	10	10	10	10	10	10	10	10	10	10	10	10	10
SUVs	60	30	29	29	26	25	24	24	23	23	23	22	22	21	21	20	20	19	18	18

Table 2.4. Inventory and Purchasing Information

Item	Initial on hand	Order conditions	Lead time	On order
Assembled small engine	150		1 day	
Assembled large engine	15		1 day	
Assembled wheels	1200		1 day	
Assembled doors	1000		1 day	
Engine–small	100	Each	3 days	
Engine–large	40	Each	4 days	
Chassis–Sedan	80	Each	2 days	
Chassis–Roadster	50	Each	2 days	30 in day 2
Chassis–Town car	30	Each	3 days	20 in day 2, 10 in day 3
Chassis–SUV	80	Each	3 days	20 in day 1, 30 in day 3
Battery	173	Multiples of 12	2 day	
Wheel	1000	200 minimum	2 days	
Windshield	250	50 minimum	2 days	
Door	1200	Multiples of 400	1 day	
Hood	150	50 minimum	1 day	
Rim	200	Multiples of 200	2 days	
Tire	300	Multiples of 144	1 day	
Lock	112	Multiples of 1000	1 day	
Handle	332	576 minimum	2 days	
Window	138	50 minimum	1 day	

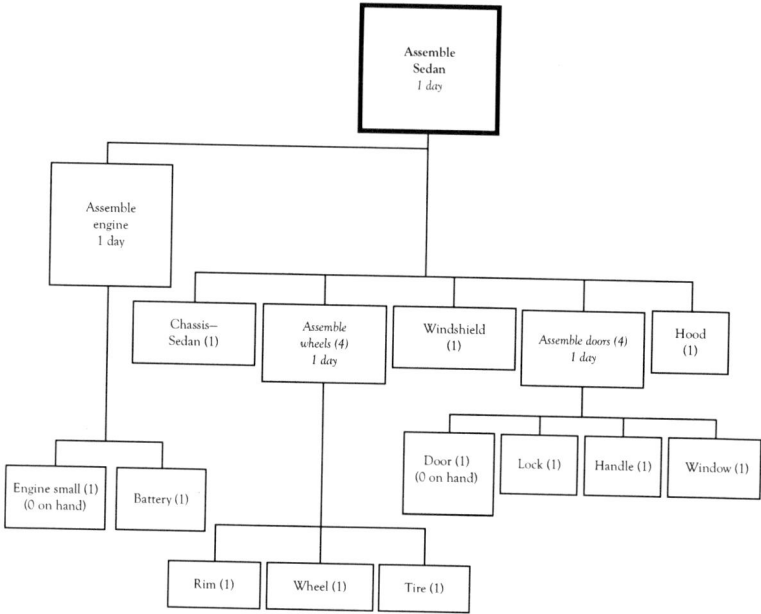

Figure 2.1. BOM for sedans.

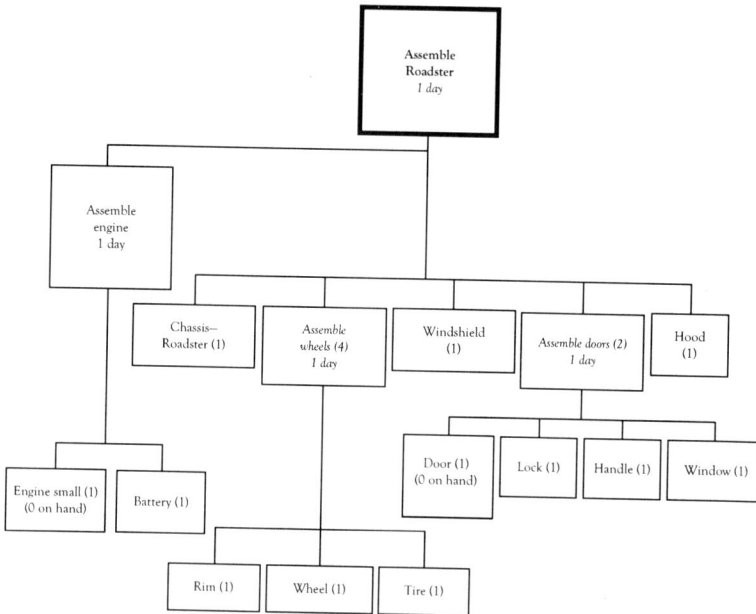

Figure 2.2. BOM for roadsters.

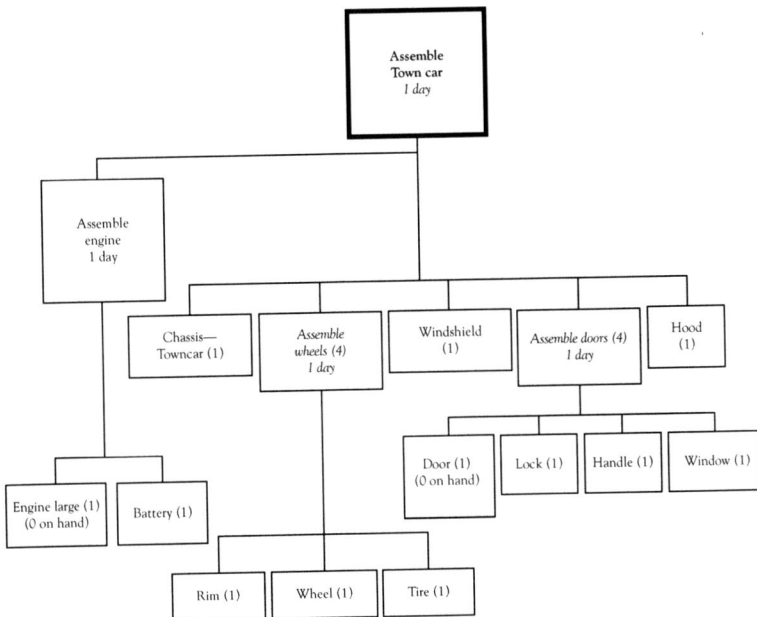

Figure 2.3. BOM for town cars.

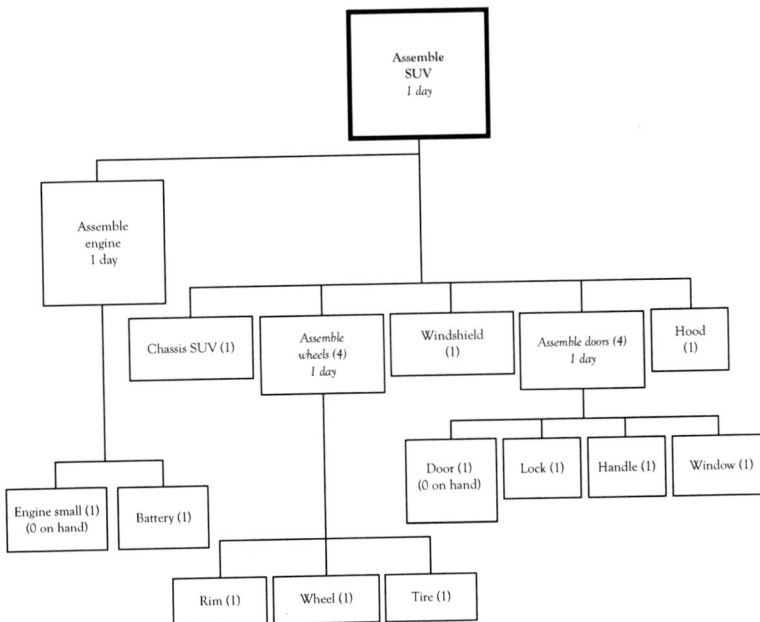

Figure 2.4. BOM for SUVs.

Vehicles are assembled with the appropriate chassis, engine, wheels, windshield, and doors. Assembly of vehicles takes one day: Materials are received ready for use at the beginning of the day (lead time includes unpacking and preparation).

Engines, wheels, and doors are subassemblies. Each of these subassemblies takes one day.

- When an engine is received, a battery is inserted to make an assembled engine.
- When a wheel is received, a rim and tire are added, making an assembled wheel.
- When a door is received, a lock, handle, and window are added, making an assembled door.

Parts needed at the beginning of each day for assembly of each vehicle, shown in Table 2.5.

Table 2.5. Top-Level Quantities Required

Assemble Sedan		Day 1	Day 2	Day 3	Day 4	Day 5	Day 6	Day 7	Day 8	Day 9	Day 10
Small engine assembly	1 ea	40	30	30	30	25	25	25	25	20	20
Chassis–Sedan	1 ea	40	30	30	30	25	25	25	25	20	20
Wheel assembly	4 ea	160	120	120	120	100	100	100	100	80	80
Windshield	1 ea	40	30	30	30	25	25	25	25	20	20
Door assembly	4 ea	160	120	120	120	100	100	100	100	80	80
Hood	1 ea	40	30	30	30	25	25	25	25	20	20

Table 2.5. Top-Level Quantities Required

Assemble Roadster		Day 1	Day 2	Day 3	Day 4	Day 5	Day 6	Day 7	Day 8	Day 9	Day 10
Small engine assembly	1 ea	15	18	17	13	15	16	14	14	13	13
Chassis–Roadster	1 ea	15	18	17	13	15	16	14	14	13	13
Wheel assembly	4 ea	60	72	68	52	60	64	56	56	52	52
Windshield	1 ea	15	18	17	13	15	16	14	14	13	13
Door assembly	2 ea	30	36	34	26	30	32	28	28	26	26
Hood	1 ea	15	18	17	13	15	16	14	14	13	13

Assemble Town car		Day 1	Day 2	Day 3	Day 4	Day 5	Day 6	Day 7	Day 8	Day 9	Day 10
Large engine assembly	1 ea	10	10	10	10	10	10	10	10	10	10
Chassis–Town car	1 ea	10	10	10	10	10	10	10	10	10	10
Wheel assembly	4 ea	40	40	40	40	40	40	40	40	40	40
Windshield	1 ea	10	10	10	10	10	10	10	10	10	10
Door assembly	4 ea	40	40	40	40	40	40	40	40	40	40
Hood	1 ea	10	10	10	10	10	10	10	10	10	10

Assemble SUV		Day 1	Day 2	Day 3	Day 4	Day 5	Day 6	Day 7	Day 8	Day 9	Day 10
Small engine assembly	1 ea	60	30	29	29	26	25	24	24	23	23
Chassis–SUV	1 ea	60	30	29	29	26	25	24	24	23	23
Wheel assembly	4 ea	240	120	116	116	104	100	96	96	92	92
Windshield	1 ea	60	30	29	29	26	25	24	24	23	23
Door assembly	4 ea	240	120	116	116	104	100	96	96	92	92
Hood	1 ea	60	30	29	29	26	25	24	24	23	23

Requirements can be aggregated across all vehicles (Table 2.6).

The MRP analysis for each of these elements can then be conducted, for instance, for small engines (Table 2.7).

This tells the assembly operation that 43 small engines need to be assembled on Day 1. The MRP analysis is conducted each time period, or daily, because there might be many changes in demand, receipts, or inventory on hand. The only action taken is for Day 1. If, as is the case here, items are ordered lot-for-lot (L4L in inventory code), the rest of the time period data can be calculated and treated as a forecast of future demands. However, as we will demonstrate, if ordering complications arise (orders come in multiples of some value or with some minimum order), they will become scheduled receipts in subsequent analyses. You can't update this particular day's MRP form, because that will create a cycle. (This little problem can be solved in many ways, but for our purposes it is sufficient to treat MRP as a time-period by time-period calculation.)

Table 2.6. Aggregated Part Requirements

		Day 1	Day 2	Day 3	Day 4	Day 5	Day 6	Day 7	Day 8	Day 9	Day 10
Assembled small engine	1 ea	115	78	76	72	66	66	63	63	56	56
Assembled large engine	1 ea	10	10	10	10	10	10	10	10	10	10
Chassis–Sedan	1 ea	40	30	30	30	25	25	25	25	20	20
Chassis–Roadster	1 ea	15	18	17	13	15	16	14	14	13	13
Chassis–Town car	1 ea	10	10	10	10	10	10	10	10	10	10
Chassis–SUV	1 ea	60	30	29	29	26	25	24	24	23	23
Assembled wheels	1 ea	500	352	344	328	304	304	292	292	264	264
Windshield	1 ea	125	88	86	82	76	76	73	73	66	66
Assembled doors	1 ea	470	316	310	302	274	272	264	264	238	238
Hood	1 ea	125	88	86	82	76	76	73	73	66	66

Table 2.7. Small Engine MRP Worksheet for Day 1

Assembled small engine	Order info	Day 1	Day 2	Day 3	Day 4	Day 5	Day 6	Day 7	Day 8	Day 9	Day 10
Gross Requirements		115	78	76	72	66	66	63	63	56	56
Scheduled receipts											
On Hand	150	35									
Net requirements	L4L		43	76	72	66	66	63	63	56	56
Planned order release	1 day lead	43	76	72	66	66	63	63	56	56	

The schedule for assembling large engines is outlined in Table 2.8.

Plant management needs to know that five large engines need to be assembled on Day 1.

Knowing the planned order release for assembled small engines and assembled large engines now allows us to proceed down the bills of material to identify subcomponents that need to be ordered. (Assembled small engines consist of one small engine and one battery, while assembled large engines consist of one large engine and one battery.) The planned order release for the higher-level component becomes the gross requirement for the subcomponents (multiplied by the number each).

Table 2.8. Large Engine MRP Worksheet for Day 1

Assembled large engine	Order info	Day 1	Day 2	Day 3	Day 4	Day 5	Day 6	Day 7	Day 8	Day 9	Day 10
Gross requirements		10	10	10	10	10	10	10	10	10	10
Scheduled receipts											
On hand	15	5									
Net requirements	L4L		5	10	10	10	10	10	10	10	10
Planned order release	1 day lead	5	10	10	10	10	10	10	10	10	-

Table 2.9. MRP Worksheets for Engines

Engine–small	Order info	Day 1	Day 2	Day 3	Day 4	Day 5	Day 6	Day 7	Day 8	Day 9	Day 10
Gross requirements		43	76	72	66	66	63	63	56	56	-
Scheduled receipts											
On hand	100	80	50	20							
Net requirements	L4L				5	25	25	25	20	20	-
Planned order release	3 day lead	5	25	25	25	20	20	-	-	-	-

Engine–large	Order info	Day 1	Day 2	Day 3	Day 4	Day 5	Day 6	Day 7	Day 8	Day 9	Day 10
Gross requirements		5	10	10	10	10	10	10	10	10	-
Scheduled receipts											
On hand	40	35	25	15	5						
Net requirements	L4L					5	10	10	10	10	-
Planned order release	4 day lead	5*	10	10	10	10	-	-	-	-	-

*The planned order release for Day 1 is the action item, identifying the need to place an order. Other day planned order releases will await more current information tomorrow.

The number of batteries to order depends on the demand for both engines. The sum of planned order releases for both small and large engines becomes the gross requirements for batteries (Table 2.10).

Table 2.10. MRP Worksheet for Batteries

Batteries	Order info	Day 1	Day 2	Day 3	Day 4	Day 5	Day 6	Day 7	Day 8	Day 9	Day 10
Gross requirements		48	86	82	76	76	73	73	66	66	-
Scheduled receipts											
On hand	173	125	69								
Net requirements	X12			13	76	76	73	73	66	66	-
Planned order release	2 day lead	24									

Here the cycling complication can be demonstrated. The batteries on hand will cover demand through Day 2, and all but 13 required on Day 3. A 2-day lead time means that orders must be placed in Day 1 to cover at least 13 batteries. But batteries have to be ordered by the dozen. One dozen (12 batteries) would be insufficient. Therefore, two dozen (24 batteries) are ordered. On the next day's MRP form, these 24 batteries would show up as scheduled receipts on what is now day 3. At that time, this will cover the demand for batteries for that day, and we can see that 11 of these batteries will be carried forward to what is now day 4, leaving a net requirement of (76 − 11 = 65) 65 batteries, which will in turn trigger an order for 72 batteries (the nearest dozen covering 65). Therefore, we will only worry about planned order releases for the current day.

Advance Planning Systems

Advanced planning systems (APSs) to aid supply chain material flows have been developed.[8] They can be obtained independently from an ERP, added on to an ERP, or found as modules within an ERP. Major ERP vendors have added APS modules. These systems offer support to meet the need to quickly and efficiently plan and control supply chains in dynamic environments. They consider resource capacities and can handle multiple sites and transportation links, offering near-optimal plans over the entire supply chain, and have the ability to identify bottlenecks. APSs may include modules to support the following:

- Supply network design through demand planning
- Supply chain planning to include purchasing and materials planning
- Demand management and forecasting
- Production planning and scheduling
- Distribution and transportation planning
- Execution to include order release, shop floor control, vehicle dispatch, and order management

APSs have been credited with enabling planners to better visualize what they could make given constraints for specific operations, ranging from shop-floor conditions to warehousing constraints and transportation system limits under conditions of specific demand requirements. They have enabled much more efficient service in meeting changing customer demand under conditions of rapidly changing prices. APSs enable changing plans rapidly, providing what-if analysis to change product mix.

Industry cases demonstrate conditions under which APSs have prospered and when they have failed.[9] The more uncertainty in the process, the greater the challenge of keeping human participation needed to make the systems work. Human interaction was found to be needed, as relying on autonomous APSs has led to problems.

The following case demonstrates some of what an APS does and how it can enable better management of a supply chain.

Advanced Planning Systems in Swedish Seed Distribution

The Swedish Farmers Supply and Crop Marketing Association is a producer cooperative providing marketing, distribution, sales, processing, and supply to about 30,000 farmers in Sweden. Prior to 2001, Swedish farmers relied on local and regional cooperatives for seed supplies. These were merged into the Association in 2001 into 13 geographic areas to provide farmers with seed, fertilizers, feed, and other required materials. The Association also sells what is produced. They have about 13,000 employees and market food to 19 countries.

The Association handles the entire seed supply chain, beginning with cleansing raw seed before packing and distribution, and deals with 270 items (including different package sizes), delivering about 4,000 tons of seed a week during the planting season.

A major restructuring of the seed supply chain was conducted in 2004. Two of six production plants were closed, along with two of four central warehouses. This resulted in lower production and storage capacity, thus increasing requirements on the transportation system. The Association supply chain consisted is illustrated in Figure 2.5.

The Association controlled production and storage facilities. Transportation was outsourced but needed assignment information with about 2 weeks of lead time.

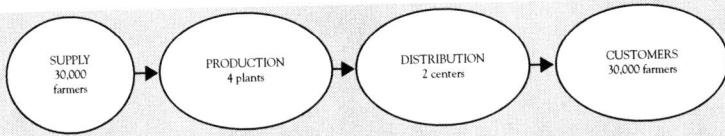

Figure 2.5. Association seed supply chain.

A Lawson M3 Supply Chain Planning (SCP) system was implemented in 2004. The system was viewed as a decision support system. The system balanced supply and demand for each weekly time period during the planning horizon (the remainder of the planting season). This is similar to the MRP planning horizon. Input data were forecasts (as in MRP); customer orders (realized demands); raw material available (inventory data); and capacities in terms of production, warehouse storage, and transportation. Forecasts were generated by the annual budget and were only updated twice per year. Actual customer orders were used for the first 2 weeks of the planning horizon. Capacity and raw material data were obtained from the Association's ERP system and fed into the Lawson M3 SCP system. Production and inventory levels were matched with capacity for each period, considering the four production and two warehouse facilities. Linear and mixed-integer programming was used by the M3 SCP to minimize cost over the overall supply chain system, with simulations conducted based on the generated solutions.

A four-phase iterative planning system was used. In the first phase, an unconstrained master plan was established to see where resources were overloaded. This would be much the same as the MRP system described earlier. The second phase took this output and reran the system adding constrained production, especially for seed cleansing and packaging capacities considering minimum batch sizes to avoid expensive start-ups. This yielded a plan for the number of shifts required at each production facilities. The third phase added limits on warehouse capacities, and new solutions were generated. To this point, unlimited transportation capacity was assumed. The fourth and final phase added transportation constraints.

Use of the system streamlined production and distribution. Total costs were decreased about 13% annually despite increasing the quantity of goods sold. A more precise measure of value added was a reduction of total cost per ton by about 15%. The use of the APS resulted in increased production batch sizes because production was centralized to four rather than six plants. Transportation costs increased slightly because more direct distribution was used, adding to overall system efficiency. Less capital was required for inventory due to better system throughput. Total planning time was reduced through the APS, with increased control of material flows.

Source: Adapted from Rudberg and Thulin (2009).

Conclusion

A variety of types of software are available to support supply chain management. The most important functions are forecasting, planning, and control of materiel throughout the system. MRP is a system designed to take forecasts and use them to control materiel in assembly operations. It requires a relatively stable operating environment in order to be effective (lots of change in actual demand versus forecasted demand causes negates many of the benefits of reduced inventory).

Advanced planning systems are focused on supply chain activities of forecasting, sourcing, and monitoring inventory. As such, they deal with the key processes related to supply chains only. They can be obtained stand-alone, added on to an ERP from an outside vendor, or obtained as a module within an ERP, at least from the larger ERP vendors.

ERP systems are rarely obtained with all available modules. Not every organization needs every module vendors have available. Even if a client might be able to use some particular module, they may not find it cost-effective and can reduce their ERP licensing and maintenance costs by eliminating marginally effective modules. The module system makes it possible to tailor ERP systems to particular organizational needs.

One of the most important modules for manufacturing involves MRP functionality. As with APS, MRP software can be obtained stand-alone, added on to an ERP from an outside vendor, or obtained as a module within an ERP.

While having the ability to choose specific modules provides flexibility, it also complicates matters. Chapter 3 will discuss optional forms of supply chain information system support in greater detail.

CHAPTER 3

Supply Chain Management Software Options

In the past, organizations typically developed their own software using their own in-house programmers and staff. This led to development of many useful but diverse and unconnected legacy systems. During the past few decades, many software vendors have focused on developing software for specific applications, creating many specific software products, to include materials requirements planning (MRP) systems, advanced planning systems (APS), and enterprise requirements planning (ERP) systems. Thus the software field has evolved from each organization creating its own software to a vendor system selling off-the-shelf packages. An even later development has been open-source software products.

Options

There are many approaches to provide information systems to support supply chains. The most well-known are SAP and Oracle. There are many other commercial vendors as well. And commercial vendor software is by no means the only source of software to manage supply chains. There are application service providers, and organizations can develop their own systems in-house (although as we will stress, this involves a lot of work). The primary categories of options to obtain supply chain support are the following:

- A custom system developed in-house
- A stand-alone advanced planning system
- A full vendor ERP system
- Selected vendor modules
- A customized vendor ERP system
- A best-of-breed approach

- Application service providers
- An open-source system

Customized Systems Developed In-House

The traditional (and very much outdated) approach is to develop software using only in-house assets. This approach does offer the greatest opportunity to gain competitive advantage. However, creating in-house software on this scale is a very difficult information systems project. Developing a strong advanced planning system in-house calls for hiring a great deal of expertise that cannot hope to compete with vendors specializing in a particular software product. The ideal way to develop an integrated system is to combine it with extensive business process reengineering (which we will discuss in chapter 4), identify the best way to do everything, and then build the computer system to accomplish this. This is a very slow and expensive way to obtain supply chain software. Yet this approach is the most flexible and responsive to organizational needs.

Stand-Alone Advanced Planning Systems (APSs)

Stand-alone APS software was presented in chapter 2 and is widely available. This will be quite a bit less costly than a vendor ERP system but will only provide specific planning support for supply chain operations. It would make a great deal of sense to integrate an APS with financial, accounting, and other organizational computing. This integration is the essence of an ERP system.

The simplest option (and by far the most expensive) is to adopt a full vendor ERP product. This is the option that vendors will suggest, and it has some strong advantages, especially with respect to relative time and installation.

Full Vendor ERP Systems

SAP and Oracle have become world leaders in software, both offering very powerful systems capable of supporting multinational organizations. But they are expensive. While SAP and Oracle contend to offer products suitable to small business organizations, they really aren't interested in talking to organizations without multimillion-dollar annual information system budgets. There also are many hidden costs, including heavy consulting fees, annual maintenance contracts, unexpectedly large training costs, and complications from changing how employees do their jobs.

There are many competitive vendors to SAP and Oracle. One notable vendor is Microsoft, offering Great Plains ERP software at a price clearly targeted to reach intermediate-sized organizations (with annual information system budgets around a million dollars). Additionally, there are many other smaller vendors, making the vendor choice for small- to intermediate-sized organizations very interesting (and complicated). Generally, you pay for what you get. But not everyone needs the computing power suitable for Exxon.

Selected Vendor Modules

Compromise systems are available. Most firms adopt only a few modules of vendor software. This is a partial form of an ERP system, which has the relative advantages of minimizing organizational risk and expenditure in the short run and minimizing the trauma of incorporating the ERP system into organizational operations. The disadvantage is that the full functionality of the vendor system is not obtained, and users still must conform to the procedures that the vendor programmed into the system.

Customized Vendor ERP Systems

Many companies adopt another hybrid approach, customizing a vendor software product. This gains flexibility over simply adopting the vendor system but risks loss of the efficiencies built into the system through best practices. This approach has the advantage of retaining core company competencies, or methods that the organization does very well, along with some of the advantages of integrated systems. There is much less negative impact on how employees do their jobs. However, it makes the IT staff work much harder and spend a great deal more money.

Best-of-Breed Approaches

The best-of-breed approach is similar to selecting a few vendor modules. Each vendor has developed a reputation for some specific ERP function. Modules considered to be competitively strong are selected from multiple vendors. Dial, a manufacturer of soap and other products, at one time had a mix of applications from Siebel, Oracle, Manugistics, and other sources.[1] Using the best-of-breed approach, custom interfaces can be developed using in-house information system development assets. Overall, however, it usually creates more trouble than it's worth.

Application Service Providers (ASPs)

You can in effect rent an ERP system through an application service provider (ASP). This is a form of outsourcing. Dial reorganized its IT and installed an SAP suite run by Electronic Data Systems (EDS) to replace Dial's 50 IT employees, who were to be transferred to EDS after an 18-month, $35 million project. Only a small governance team was retained by Dial, with the purpose of dealing with IT strategy, architecture, and industry applications. Overall expenses for the transfer were expected to be $110 million. Outsourcing is attractive to many types of organizations but especially to those that have small IT staffs, without expertise in enterprise systems. The primary benefit of an ASP is that the using organization doesn't have to worry about system development, nor about being at the mercy of vendors when they make changes to their software. Some organizations, such as General Motors, have outsourced all their IT operations.[2] However, the risk is simply transferred, because the user is now subject to the mercy of the ASP. The decision is very similar to that of deciding to buy or rent housing. In the long run, you are usually better off buying a house. However, the cash flow impact and risk avoidance of renting is much better than buying.

Open-Source ERP Systems

Another major development in ERP has been open software systems. The open software idea was made famous by the Linux operating system. There are many nuances to definitions, but we will use the term *open source* for software distributed without charge. A related idea is software as a service (SaaS), involving web distribution of bits of software capable of doing particular functions, at a fee. Open-source software provides the opportunity to utilize more service-oriented systems, strongly supported by organizations such as IBM with their on-demand computing initiative and an industry focus on SaaS, where vendors develop software posted to the web and made available for customer use. Web delivery has been selected as a means to distribute a number of interesting enterprise system software, led by Compiere from France. Compiere and many similar products are not open source in the sense that users can modify the code. They are open in the sense that they are downloadable for free. The business model is based on collecting fees for service and support.

The first six means of obtaining supply chain software support listed so far are fairly traditional. We will elaborate a bit on two relatively unique approaches: outsourcing and open source.

Outsourcing Supply Chain Management Software

There are risks in outsourcing. In many cases, costs rise precipitously after the outsourcing firm has become committed to the relationship. These tradeoffs are recapitulated in Table 3.1.

Table 3.1. Factors for and Against Outsourcing

Reasons to outsource	Reasons against outsourcing
Reduced capital expenditure for software and updates	Security and privacy concerns
Lower costs gained through ASP and economies of scale (efficiency)	Concern about vendor dependency and lock-in
More flexible and agile IT capability	Availability, performance, and reliability concerns
Increased service levels at reasonable cost	High migration costs
Expertise availability unaffordable in-house (eliminate the need to recruit IT personnel)	Expertise is a competency critical to organizational success
Allowing the organization to focus on their core business.	Systems are inextricably tied to IT infrastructure
Continuous access to the latest technology	Some key applications may be in-house and critical
Reduced risk of infrastructure failure	Operations are currently as efficient as the ASPs
Manage IT workload variability	Corporate culture doesn't deal well with working with partners.
Replace obsolete systems	

Source: Bryson and Sullivan (2003); "ERP outsourcing" (2003); Clymer (2004); Olson (2004).

One risk is that an ASP might shirk its commitments due to bankruptcy or for other reasons. ASP sites might also be attacked and vandalized, or destroyed by natural disaster. Each organization must balance these factors and make their own decisions. The case studies in this chapter demonstrate how two organizations reached different conclusions.

ERP is only one service offered through ASPs. Acquisition of supply chain management systems such as an advanced planning system through an application service provider often makes sense.

Open-Source Supply Chain Software

Open-source development has proven highly successful in general software product development. Red Hat claims that open-source software (OSS) can save businesses money by

1. Enabling use of commodity hardware rather than proprietary machines
2. Avoiding expensive maintenance contracts
3. Obtaining greater functionality, reliability, and performance
4. Increasing productivity through a faster learning curve and availability of support tools
5. Avoiding vendor lock-in
6. Reducing the need for specialized security consultants and tools

Open-source software is thus becoming a viable alternative to proprietary software, with an obvious cost advantage. There are risks, in that one cannot expect the same level of service with OSS as with proprietary alternatives. However, support for many OSS products is available, from such organizations as IBM and Red Hat. Contemporary software selection thus requires considering the tradeoffs between open-source and proprietary software. Open-source ERP products include Compiere, OpenMFG, Open For Business Project, Tiny ERP, Open Office, and OpenPro, each providing various levels of enterprise information system functionality in various forms of open-source relationships. The open-source project center Sourceforge.net had over 1,000 ERP projects ongoing as of May 7, 2009.

ERP systems have evolved to expansion of functionality, especially in the form of customer relationship management (CRM) and supply chain support, to a transformed product often referred to as enterprise information systems (EISs) as discussed in chapter 1. Recently, ERP vendors have realized that open-source systems have capabilities, both as a source of content for vendors and as a threat to the proprietary enterprise system market share from competitors based on OSS development or delivery. Open-source ERP products can provide flexibility and of course have the advantage of free software access. As ERPs are commonly implemented by organizations, it is hard to attain competitive advantage through implementation of an ERP product. OSS ERP systems can be an answer for competitive advantages since organizations are able to customize their information systems by modifying the open software codes. Three potential benefits in using OSS ERP systems are increased adaptability, decreased reliance on a single supplier, and reduced costs.

Comparison of Supply Chain Management Software Sources

Table 3.2 compares advantages and disadvantages of some representative points on a continuum.

Table 3.2. Advantages and Disadvantages of Alternative Software Sources

Method	Advantages	Disadvantages
Customized systems developed in-house	Best fit with organizational needs	Most difficult to develop Most expensive Slowest
Stand-alone APSs	Less expenditure Much simpler installation	Harder to integrate with other applications
Full vendor ERP products	Relatively fast Less expensive than customization Efficient from an IT perspective Easier to upgrade	Inflexible Make employees change work methods
Selected vendor modules	Less risk Relatively fast Least expensive vendor approach	If expanding, long run time and higher costs
Customized vendor ERP systems	Retain flexibility while keeping vendor expertise	Slower Usually more expensive
Best-of-breed approach	Theoretically gain best of all systems	Difficult to link modules Slow Need middleware
Application service providers	Least risk Least cost Fastest Least subject to vendor change	At the mercy of ASP No control Subject to price increases
Open-source systems	COST! (acquisition is free) Flexible	Greatest risk (other than in-house) Need employees with ability to link open-source systems

We will conclude this chapter with a case study of a small organization's experience in obtaining inexpensive software support for their made-to-order planning operation.

Implementation of an Open-Source ERP System

WETI (fictitious name of a real firm) is a small enterprise that manufactures industrial automated welding systems for several industries. As the client base expanded the required inventory to service the many uniquely engineered to order systems expanded as well. Customer service for repair and replacement parts also became a large part of daily operations. Demand for systems increased, the number of engineers grew and the subsequent paper trail exploded. There was a need for a system to manage orders, scheduling, billing, and inventory.

Business Case: First Round

Company production increased 500% in the first 2 years and steadily increased at about 20% each year thereafter. Early in 2003 it was recognized that the old way of keeping track of sales, parts, and documentation was not adequate to keep up with the demand of its customers. They began to explore several information systems, including but not limited to the following:

- In-house development
- High-cost vendor software ERP systems
- Low-cost vendor systems
- Off-the-shelf software such as QuickBooks and Microsoft Office Suite

In-house development was an option, considering the companies experience in software engineering, but the limiting factor that prevented development was time and manpower. Several midmarket ERP software providers were considered, such as Microsoft Great Plains, Sage software, and Infor ERP Visual. After several months of moving through the typical sales routine, proposals were given to WETI, and based on the average implementation cost of $60,000, all were rejected. The owners felt that at that price it would be worth reconsidering in-house development. Both owners had come from larger companies and had seen some of the horrors of vendor ERP implementation. They felt that the high cost was not justified or worth the headache of drastically conforming to a system that would lock them into ongoing support and maintenance costs for the life of the software, as is typical of traditional ERP software vendors.

First Round Choice: ERPlite

The employee in charge of finding a software solution examined low-cost ERP systems available at that time. ERPlite (http://www.erplite. com) was selected. The price per user was around $300 at the time, which was drastically lower than the prices offered by the traditional ERP vendors. Furthermore, the software seemed that it would meet many of the requirements needed for their ERP system, to include e-business, inventory and MRP, and accounting.

At the price and perceived functionality the decision to move forward with ERPlite was easy for the owners to accept. The risks seemed very manageable, and if the system failed to deliver the loss would be minimal. In mid-2004, three user seats were purchased, with the intent to buy more once the basics were in place and functioning well. The three seats were installed, and everything worked well for a couple of months. Testing went smoothly, but regardless some limitations were discovered. The processing of work orders for the volume of work that WETI was experiencing not only took a long time to compile but also created an overwhelming amount of paper trail.

Tradeoffs

As the ERPlite system was altered to accommodate WETI's unique problems, it became more difficult for ERPlite staff to provide effective over-the-phone support, but not due to their lack of effort. Within a year WETI decided to forgo monthly support and decided it would pay on a per-instance basis if further support were needed. Along with the cancellation of monthly support, they no longer would receive bug fixes or patches created by ERPlite. Within 18 months of installation the head of the manufacturing staff decided that the work order system was not adequate to keep up with their requirements, and they stopped using the official work order system.

Results: First Round

Four years later the only functional aspects of ERPlite being used were the purchasing module and sales quotes module. Purchasing would use the stored product numbers, its preferred supplier, and the most recent purchase price to generate purchase orders. Historical purchase orders were stored in the database and could be accessed for historical changes in price or to list a set of purchased products associated with a particular project or product build. Sales would use the system to determine a sales price based on a standard markup of the purchase price. The items could be added to a sales quote and sent via fax or e-mail to a customer. It should be noted that sales quotes were only used for spare and placement parts only, not for entire systems sales. Purchase orders and sales quote were generated and then printed to provide accounting with the information necessary to generate a check from accounts payable or an invoice from accounts receivable within QuickBooks. This duplication of effort was common in many areas of WETI's daily business operations.

Round Two: Midmarket ERP Vendors Versus Open-Source ERP

The business case in this round proceeded much as in the first round. This time, however, those in charge of finding the replacement for ERPlite started with low-cost solutions first, looking at programs such as DBA Manufacturing (htttp://www.dbamanufacturing.com) and Fishbowl Inventory (http://www.fishbowlinventory.com). These low-cost solutions were tested through free trials, and while robust and very functional, there were concerns voiced over some key limitations regarding WETI's mode of operations.

Alternatives Considered

Over the period of 3 months, several ERP vendors were evaluated including but not limited to the following:

- Sage AccPac
- Epicor
- Made2Manage
- E2 Shop System
- Exact JobBoss
- Infor Global's Visual
- M1 by Bowen and Groves (now ECi M1)

The selection was narrowed to Visual and M1. They both seemed to offer a comprehensive solution for an engineer-to-order (ETO) or made-to-order (MTO) manufacturing operation. After another couple of months of demonstrations with various employees of WETI and more importantly with the owners, it was decided to call for proposals for a 10-user system with on-site implementation support and training for several end users. The bids ranged from $18,000 to about $42,000 with approximately an additional $5,000 to $8,000 expense on a dedicated server and SQL database software. The owners balked at the price, and it was quickly realized on all sides that the owners had no intention of purchasing a system at that point in time. The company had just built a state-of-the-art manufacturing center and were heavily invested in the development of a new automation product that was over budget and past the hoped-for completion time, and this overshadowed any potential gain that would be realized from a purchased ERP system.

xTuple

Information was being entered two or three times into the legacy "systems" that each department had developed, mostly in Excel. After about 3 weeks had passed from the decision to forgo the traditional ERP, the head engineer approached those involved with the ERP selection process and mentioned that his friend in a research and development arm of a major company was using a program called xTuple to keep track of procurement, production, and costs. They were using xTuple in conjunction with their company's large vendor ERP system to keep track of each project's inputs and outputs, because the large ERP program was only doing so from a macro view (simply keeping track of the overall departments parts and costs). WETI's head of engineering and manufacturing was excited about the product and helped others see how it might be a viable solution for the company's many ERP needs.

xTuple Implementation

After a quick overview of the xTuple website, the Postbooks installer was downloaded through sourceforge.net via the xTuple Postbooks project page. In addition to the source code, an SQL database was also needed. All the installation information, including information regarding the SQL database installation was available on the xTuple website. PostgreSQL is the open-source database that xTuple installs with.

Installation was easy, and in a matter of minutes the software was loaded and functional in the most basic form. There was no data available, but the entire system was there to alter and test. There were a few database options to choose from on the Sourceforge Postbooks project page. In addition to the empty database, there is also the quick start database, which contains a basic chart of accounts and also the account assignments required to run a full range of transactions common to most businesses. In addition there is a demo database that contains the accounting data found in the quick start database and a set of sample data such as parts, accounting chart of accounts, bill of materials (BOM) data, and so on. For initial demonstration and testing purposes the demo database was loaded.

The initial assessment of the Postbooks edition of xTuple only lasted a few days by the two-person team in charge of finding and implementing ERP for WETI. It was found to be very capable and easy to use. In addition to the ERP software, xTuple also offered a free SQL report writer called OpenRPT. This feature provides a very functional tool to query the PostgreSQL database for information and reports such as sales quotes, work orders, purchase orders, inventory reports, accounting information, and so forth. This additional component was explored further in an effort to modify or create reports that would give manufacturing, accounting, and purchasing the data in a form that they were familiar with, as to lessen implementation pains and also to better mold the ERP program into a product that would closely match the way WETI like to run their company.

After about a month of this segmented testing, it was decided to go ahead with a more structured implementation of the ERP system. Item master data was added in batches as it was formatted and arranged in a matter that suited the structure of the program and the use requirements of WETI. This went slowly due to the unstructured format that the data was in and because of the lack of information for a large number of items. Most of the parts being added were part of BOMs for products that had never been tracked electronically. Many of those major products and their subcomponents needed part numbers and names, which added considerably to the time it took to organize the data into a form that could be used by xTuple. Within a few weeks there were approximately 750 to 1,000 parts out of over 16,000 entered into the Postbooks database.

The open platform also allowed for modification of the functions and reports found in the core software. This allows companies to mold the software around some of the business practices that provide a competitive advantage while also providing the benefits of a fully integrated ERP program and the best practices most ERP software is based on.

Overall, open-source ERP software has been proven a capable solution for many businesses throughout the world. While it may not account for a large percentage of market share, there is demand for such solutions, and small business can gain many advantages from the adoption of such software. Open-source software isn't always free, but most companies do offer a no-cost version of their software, with an upgrade path when more functionality is needed.

Source: D. L. Olson and J. Staley (2012).

Conclusion

There are many ways to obtain supply chain software support. Specialty products such as advanced planning systems are available. However, this functionality is available in almost every ERP vendor system, with the added benefit of integrating organizational computing. The amount of money required to obtain software licenses is considerable, making it very important for organizations to conduct a sound business case analysis. This isn't easy, as there are so many options available. That is undoubtedly why consultants are so often used (which by no means reduces expense!).

Two interesting options to avoid many of these pitfalls are outsourcing to ASPs or using open-source software. Outsourcing has its own risks, although a major benefit in up-front cash flow. However, outsourcing hasn't been all that popular for smaller organizations. It appears more often for major organizations such as General Motors, Xerox, or U.S. government agencies who wish to get out of the information system business and to focus on their key business operations. Open-source software has proven quite popular in Europe and South America, as well as for small organizations in the United States (especially state and local governments). These systems cannot be expected to provide all the functionality of well-tested commercial vendor products, but they offer sufficient functionality for many organizations. Installing an open-source ERP calls for a new type of information system specialist, and this market is still under development.

In chapter 4, we will look at the key task of business process reengineering, followed by a closer look at business cases in chapter 5 and software installation project management in chapter 6.

CHAPTER 4

Business Process Reengineering in Supply Chains

Michael Hammer coined the term *business process reengineering* (BPR) in 1990. Enterprise resource planning (ERP) systems depend on BPR to gain efficiency. The concept of BPR can be traced to its origins in management theories developed as early as the nineteenth century. The purpose of reengineering is to "make all your processes the best-in-class." Frederick Taylor suggested in the 1880s that managers use process reengineering methods to discover the best processes for performing work and that these processes be reengineered to optimize productivity. BPR echoes the classical belief that there is only one best way to conduct tasks. Best practices are vendor methods selected to be the best way to accomplish elemental business tasks. Accomplishing this goal depends on maximizing the effectiveness of policy development and program delivery, planning and budgetary arrangements, decision-making processes, organizational structures, workplace relations, and people management. Significant gains in performance have been attained through BPR.

BPR is suggested as a key step in the initial development of any organization's ERP. While best practices often are useful, organizations that have developed core competencies in specific functions are better served by avoiding the vendor best practices that all their competitors can buy to retain what they do well. Amazon.com undoubtedly retains processes that it developed to make it successful in e-business rather than adopt all their ERP vendor's processes.

Increasingly, information and communications technology, often in the form of an ERP, plays a vital role in determining the quality and accessibility of services. Expansion in ERP has opened the door for even greater efficiencies and enhanced service delivery through integrated processes. The strategic application of ERP opens up opportunities for even greater gains as public and private sector enterprises transform their existing processes. For individual enterprises and government agencies, the most noteworthy gains are achieved when ERP decisions are business-driven.

Processes

A process is a logical set of related activities taking inputs, adding value through doing things, to create an output. In business, there are many different ways to get work done. Information systems play a key role in providing a means to collect data, store it efficiently, generate reports to let management know what the organization is doing, and archive data for future reference as needed.

Blanket adoption of an ERP product will discard processes in which the organization has developed a competitive advantage. Instead of changing those processes, the ERP system should be modified. Other activities will be better done following the ERP system's best practices. Even here, a transition period can be expected where employees who have to radically change what they do. Productivity degradation will occur while users learn to adapt to the new system. In the long run the new system is most often better. Those who refuse to adapt to it usually have to learn new skills with their next employer.

In general processes can be divided into two broad categories. Operational processes have to do with accomplishing typical business functions, including product development, order management, and customer support. Infrastructure processes are more administrative, such as establishing and implementing strategy and managing many aspects of the organization to include human resources, physical assets, and information systems. Each of these generic processes, whether operational or relating to infrastructure, involves sets of tasks needed to accomplish work.

For example, in the operational process of order management, it is necessary to forecast the volume of demand expected for the products produced by an organization. The function of forecasting can be accomplished in many ways:

- Using last month's demand as a prediction for this month
- Using the monthly demand from a year ago as the prediction for this month

- Applying a spreadsheet algorithm such as exponential smoothing over available monthly data
- Incorporating seasonality indices into such a spreadsheet algorithm
- Taking known orders and adjusting forecasts based on past demand records
- Relying on managerial judgment
- Using guesswork (throwing darts, rolling dice, consulting a Ouija board)

Whatever the forecasting method used, it can become part of the process of determining the quantity to order each time an order is place.

A business process is what the organization does to get its work done. For instance, supply chains need to take orders from customers and contact downstream sources to create the product to fulfill orders. This process requires a number of actions. Before computer automation, this could have involved a process given in Figure 4.1.

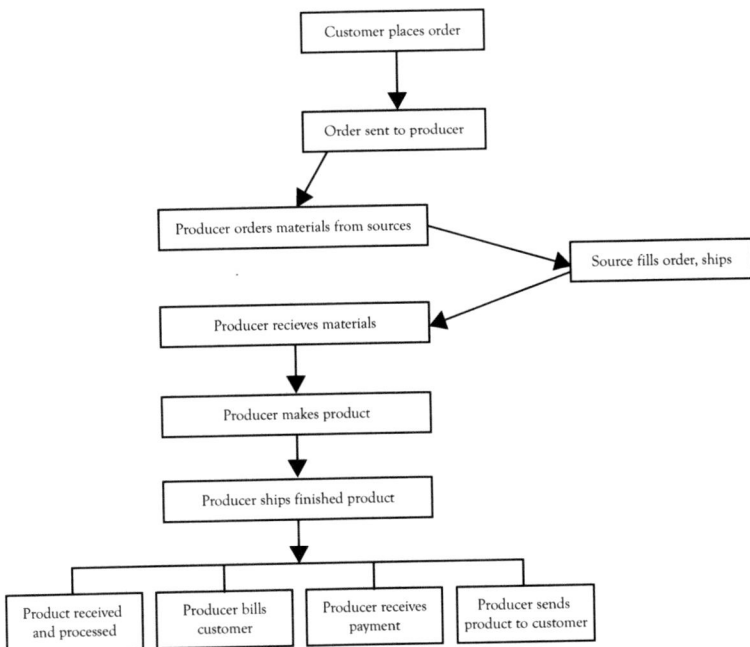

Figure 4.1. Manual business process.

The old process begins with receiving the customer order and then notifying the producer. The producer in turn then needs to notify its material sources to obtain the things needed to make the product. Often a single source was preferred, for simplicity and to reduce communication requirements. Once materials are received, the producer can proceed with production and, when completed, ship finished goods to the core supply chain organization. This organization then makes sure payment is received and, when this payment is confirmed, sends the product to the customer. The process is linear and slow and has potential for miscommunication. Keep in mind that this is a simplified supply chain and could involve many other elements.

Utilizing information technology offers many opportunities to reengineer processes, making them more efficient. A possibility is given in Figure 4.2.

Electronic automated systems can expand opportunities by reaching lower price sources from a larger pool of candidate sources. This also can reduce risk because more alternate sources are available in times of crisis, such as disruption by earthquakes, tsunamis, volcanoes, or wars. Deregulation and competition are drivers for the creation of new business models through BPR. ERP systems provide a higher level of flexibility in meeting growing customer demands, while demanding higher levels of automation and integration in almost all business processes.

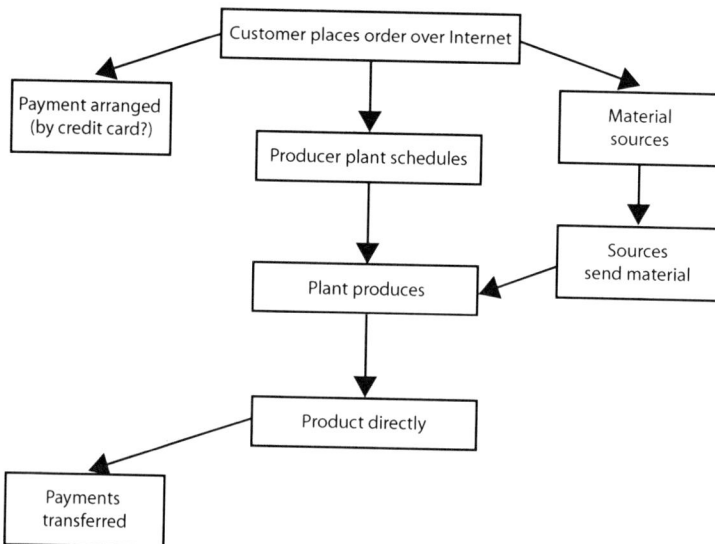

Figure 4.2. Automated business process.

The change implicit in BPR has many risks. Even advocates of BPR cite failure rates of 50 to 70%.[1] Reasons for difficulty in implementing BPR include the following:

- Employee resistance to change
- Inadequate attention to employee concerns
- Mismatch of strategies used and goals
- Lack of oversight
- Failure in leadership commitment

Best Practices

One of the primary features of the SAP ERP product has been best practices. Business process reengineering is an activity designed to identify a best practice. Once a best practice is identified that would seem applicable to most organizations, it can be incorporated into an ERP system. SAP spends considerable research efforts to identify the best way of doing conventional ERP tasks. They had 800 to 1,000 best practices included in their R/3 software.[2] Consultants often develop further specialized expertise that firms can purchase. A best practice is a method that has been judged to be superior to other methods. This implies the most efficient way to perform a task.

A related concept is benchmarking. Benchmarking is comparing an organization's methods with peer groups, with the purpose of identifying the best practices that lead to superior performance. Best practices are usually identified through the benchmarking phase of a business process reengineering activity. Best practices thus often change the organizational climate and attempt to bring about dramatic improvements in performance.

Vendors attempt to be comprehensive and to be all things to all people. But missed deadlines, excessive costs, and employee frustrations are common in the implementation of ERP. A more participative design approach could help in implementing ERP. If a client implements the entire suite of SAP modules, as well as their tools for system implementation, SAP can ensure timely implementation within budget. However, this approach disregards the human factors of the client business culture.

While business process reengineering was designed to consider human values and business purposes, these factors are clearly neglected in BPR application. Care needs to be taken to consider human factors in new processes. The human factor costs of training and obtaining cooperative participation is the key to the successful implementation of ERP.

Reengineering Options

Implementing reengineering can occur in two basic ways: either clean-slate or technology-enabled BPR. While these are not the only choices (they are the extremes of a spectrum of reengineering implementation possibilities), they are good concepts to explain the choices available in accomplishing reengineering.

Clean-Slate Reengineering

In clean-slate reengineering, everything is designed from scratch. In essence, clean-slate engineering involves reengineering, followed by selection of that software best supporting the new system design. Processes are reengineered based on identified needs and requirements of the organization. As its name implies, clean-slate reengineering has no predefined constraints. This theoretically enables design of the optimal system for the organization. This approach is more expensive than technology-enabled reengineering, but clean-slate reengineering is more responsive to organizational needs.

Clean-slate reengineering is slower and harder to apply than the technology-enabled approach to implementation. However, clean-slate reengineering offers a way to retain competitive advantages that the organization has developed. Ideally, this approach can develop the optimal system for the organization. Clean-slate reengineering can also involve significant changes in the way that the organization does business. However, the adjustment in how organization members do their business often retains the features that were found to work well in the past. Thus, while training is required, the impact is probably less than in the technology-enabled approach.

Technology-Enabled Reengineering

In technology-enabled reengineering, first the system is selected and then reengineering is conducted (constrained reengineering). The reengineering process is thus constrained by the selected system. This approach is faster and cheaper than clean-slate reengineering, because the software does not have to be changed (it is the basis of the design). Cap Gemini refers to technology-enabled reengineering as *concurrent transformation*.

The technology-enabled approach designs the organizational system around the abilities of the vendor software. SAP's best practices, for instance, are designed to do things right in the first place. If SAP's research came up with ways to do everything you do better than you used to do them, this would be the best option. It is the easiest to implement, is usually much faster to implement, and thus costs less to implement. On the negative side, it also usually involves the most change in organizational practice and thus the most complications for training. In practice, therefore, while the ERP installation project looks great from time, budget, and functionality perspectives, the actual benefits to the organization are often disappointing. Table 4.1 compares trade-offs across these approaches.

Table 4.1. Comparison of Clean-Slate and Technology-Enabled Reengineering

Clean-slate advantages	Technology-enabled advantages
Not constrained by tool limitations	Focus on ERP best practices
Not limited by completeness of best practice database	Tools help structure and focus reengineering
Company may have unique features where vendor best practices aren't appropriate	Process bounded and thus easier
Not subject to vendor software changes	Know that design is feasible
May be only way to embed processes like web, bar coding into new technology	Experience of others ensures design will work
Maintain competitive advantage	Greater likelihood of cost, time achievement
	Software available (already developed)

Clean-slate disadvantages	Technology-enabled disadvantages
No preexisting structure to design	Reengineering limited by tool
Greater likelihood of infeasibility	System evolution possibly limited by technology
May involve more consultants	System evolution may be limited by technology
May be more costly, slower	No relative advantage (others can purchase same system)
May not work with selected ERP	All best practices may not be available

Many organizations have difficulty in efforts to switch from old legacy systems to ERP. These legacy systems included distribution, financial, and customer service systems developed in-house over the years.

BPR in the Colorado Department of Transportation

The Colorado Department of Transportation (CDOT) is responsible for building and maintaining Colorado's highway construction system. Their annual operating budget is in the $1.5 billion range. CDOT utilized computer information systems for record keeping and management. However, a variety of legacy systems had been developed over the years for specific functions, and these systems were inconsistent and not integrated.

CDOT's Information Technology Office adopted a project to replace their legacy information systems, which were considered to be badly out of date. They hired CIBER, a consulting firm to assess their system. CIBER produced an Information Technology Strategic Plan for CDOT, concluding that CDOT needed an off-the-shelf ERP, at an estimated cost of $50 million. CDOT information technology leaders subsequently adopted an extensive BPR study to evaluate how candidate ERP packages would serve CDOT.

By the end of 2003, the BPR project had sufficiently progressed to enable a request for bids. Bids were received from Siemens, PeopleSoft, Oracle, and SAP. Siemens was eliminated from consideration, and PeopleSoft had been purchased by Oracle, leaving SAP and Oracle as remaining bids. The two systems were carefully scored by a committee of a dozen CDOT employees on criteria to include price, fit with needs, and ability to meet CDOT functional requirements. The committee selected the SAP bid.

Because installing an ERP has proven complex, a consulting firm experienced in SAP installation was sought. Bids in response to this request for proposal were received from three consultants. Deloitte was selected after a rigorous review process.

The SAP installation project initiated in the summer of 2004, led by a steering committee of four full-time procurement representatives plus 60 representatives of CDOT major functions. Two

SAP representatives and dozens of Deloitte consultants participated in planning as well. The CDOT project manager met daily with the CDOT chief information officer (CIO) and updated the project plan weekly. BPR addressed over 4,000 requirements for the system.

An independent verification and validation firm was hired to analyze Deloitte's processes to ensure adherence to the contract. This firm identified discrepancies that were reported to the CIO in December 2004. Concerns were expressed about defective requirements due to insufficient requirements analysis and truncated BPR efforts. There also was concern about testing and quality assurance policies used by the installation contractor. It was suggested that the ERP implementation be placed on hold until BPR issues were resolved. However, the person making this suggestion was removed from the implementation team, and the ERP implementation project continued.

The project consisted of phased introduction of specific ERP modules. The Human Resources module was scheduled to be launched on April 1, 2006, not including the payroll function. This launch succeeded. Remaining modules, including payroll, were scheduled to launch November 1, 2006. User acceptance tests were conducted before that date, and training was provided to CDOT employees. However, this training proved insufficient, and the new system extensively increased the work the CDOT employees had to do to enter payroll information. In addition to training insufficiencies, the new system was not extensively tested, and there was no recovery plan.

The case demonstrates the role of BPR in extensive software implementations. Ideally, BPR should be conducted prior to software selection and final design. Often, as appears to be the case at CDOT, BPR is not adequately conducted. A survey of CDOT staff in 2008 indicated that 60% wanted to scrap (or fix) their 1-year-old computer system.

Source: Adapted from McCubbrey and Fukami (2009).

Conclusion

BPR is an important philosophy. It aims to achieve improvements in performance by redesigning the processes through which an organization operates, maximizing their value-added content. This approach can be applied at an individual process level or to the whole organization. Business process reengineering is often a major component of an ERP installation. This implies massive changes in the way in which organizations do their business. This has great potential payoff but also implies a great deal of change in people's work lives, which requires a lot of attention to demonstrate benefits, as well as a great deal of retraining.

Requirements analysis is important in identifying what a proposed system is to do. In ERP projects, requirements analysis takes the form of business process reengineering, to identify the best way (best practice) for each business process supported by the system. Business process reengineering can be accomplished in many ways, but two ways represent the extremes. Clean-slate BPR starts from scratch and is the ideal approach. Technology-enabled BPR begins with the software selected. This is faster and less expensive, as many of the processes are selected from the system. In practice, neither extreme is necessarily best. Hammer and Stanton credited reengineering as doing a great deal of good, despite being a euphemism for mindless downsizing by some.[3] BPR has enabled companies to operate faster and more efficiently and to use information technology more productively. Employees often obtain more authority and a better understanding of the role their work plays for the organization as a whole. Customers get higher-quality products and more responsive service. Shareholders obtain larger dividends and higher stock values because BPR reduces cost and increases revenues. Executives no longer see their organizations as separate entities but instead see them as related elements in larger systems linked through information flows across the business, reaching customers and suppliers.

CHAPTER 5

System Selection

Installing supply chain management (SCM) systems, whether a stand-alone system or as a component of an enterprise resource planning (ERP) system, would seem to be a simple matter. After all, the software, while expensive, has been thoroughly tested by many customers. However, ERP implementations are consistently reported to have failure rates in excess of 60%.[1] A business case should be a key part of the process of selecting the form of supply chain software for an organization. This chapter will demonstrate fundamental means of financial analysis and show how other methods can be used to consider other factors describing expected project performance.

Cost-benefit analysis seeks to identify accurate measures of benefits and costs in monetary terms and uses the ratio of benefits to costs. Costs and benefits for software systems are inherently difficult to estimate accurately because the many uncertainties, many hidden (unexpected) costs, and potential benefits are difficult to measure precisely.

Total Cost of Ownership

Different types of cost are unique to supply chain software applications:

1. *Obvious cost*—The license cost of the software itself is the most understandable.
2. *Cost of system integration*—This is probably the single major factor in determining the long-term cost of a system. If a small company buys an inventory control and accounting system, they would want the system be interfaced with their customer relationship management (CRM) system and also to their shipping system in the warehouse. The company will also need some modifications to the central part order entry system, which interacts with customer and shipping data. Interfaces and the customization are costly and more involved with time.

3. *Cost of Implementation*—This is the cost of getting the system live in the first place. Implementation costs vary widely based on the application. Components of this cost are data migration services, systems integration, training, consulting, process engineering, and project management.

4. *Expenses of Customization*—Almost every business software implementation calls for at least some customization. As technology has advanced, the cost of customization has come down; however, this continues to be a major cost with supply chain software.

5. *Platform*—Software requires a computer platform. The older the computer platform, the higher the likelihood that a more powerful platform will be required to adequately support a new supply chain software system.

6. *Safeguarding Costs*—Maintenance to sustain the system is an ongoing annual cost. Companies often charge around 20% of the purchase price per year for this cost category.

7. *Training Costs*—Training of user personnel is critical. A period of about 1 year is usually required until the trauma of new system implementation passes. This difficult period is easier to cope with if a good, thorough training program is adopted. Managers generally tend to underestimate the magnitude required in such a training program.

Total Cost of Ownership (TCO) has long been recognized as a significant factor in supply chain software strategies and decisions. Yet while both end users and vendors tend to talk about lower TCO, and many vendors claim it as a point of differentiation, seldom do they speak in terms of specific metrics.[2]

Because supply chain systems involve long time frames (for benefits, if not for costs as well), considering the net present value of benefits and costs is important. We will start with basic cost-benefit analysis and then consider value analysis (one way to deal with subjective benefits) and a simple version of multiattribute utility theory (a means to consider trade-offs across multiple measures of value).

Cost-Benefit Example

Consider a proposed supply chain software implementation involving an implementation study in Year 1 conducted by a small team of company personnel, aided by a hired consultant at $500,000 in the first year. This is a fairly small implementation, and at this stage of the analysis, typically expected costs are underestimated. This analysis in Year 1 includes some business process reengineering and the formation of a training team. This cost analysis assumes the purchase of a $500,000 supply chain software system from a reputable vendor, with maintenance costs for patches and upgrades of $100,000 each year thereafter. Extra hardware to support the proposed system will be needed in Year 1 at $750,000. Training expense will be low in Year 1, high in Year 2, and drop thereafter. The firm wants to treat software acquisition, hardware acquisition, and consulting in the first year as an investment.

Operating the system will also incur costs. This budget is expected to be $1 million in Year 1, growing at a rate of 10% per year thereafter. The firm's cost of capital is 10%.

The board disagreed somewhat about the expected rate of growth of benefits. The dominant group on the board expects benefits from the supply chain system to be $2 million per year in Year 2, $3 million in Year 3, and to grow at 30% per year thereafter. The time horizon selected is 5 years, as new software is expected to outdate any currently available system after that time.

The board often disagreed about assumptions in cost-benefit models. A vocal minority thinks that this expectation is far too high and that benefits will only grow at the rate of 10% annual increase after Year 3. This data is summarized in Table 5.1.

Table 5.1. Cost-Benefit Analysis Input Data—Example Proposal

Year	Internal team	Consultants	Software	Hardware	Training	Benefits
1	1,000,000	500,000	500,000	750,000	500,000	
2	1,100,000		100,000		750,000	2,000,000
3	1,210,000		100,000		1,000,000	3,000,000
4	1,331,000		100,000		800,000	3,900,000
5	1,464,100		100,000		400,000	5,070,000
Totals	6,105,100	500,000	900,000	750,000	3,450,000	13,970,000

Cost-benefit analysis is somewhat arbitrary because it usually is applied considering up-front expenditure as investment, used in the denominator, with net cash flow thereafter used in the numerator. Continuing with our earlier example, investment here is the $2,150,000 spent on consultants, software acquisition, and hardware. One version of the cost-benefit ratio would thus be the following:

$$(\$13,970,000 = \$6,105,100 - \$3,450,000)/\$2,150,000 = 2.053$$

This looks like a very profitable investment, with the investment covered 2.053 times. Furthermore, the arbitrary nature of what to include as investment can be demonstrated by assigning all costs to investment (not recommended, but for purposes of demonstration):

$$\$13,970,000/(\$6,105,100 + \$500,000 + \$900,000 + \$750,000 + \$3,450,000) = 1.193$$

Here benefits still cover investment, but the ratio is much lower. Another problem is that the benefits are all in the future, while the bulk of the costs are early. Money has a time value.

Net Present Value Calculation

Net present value (NPV) is calculated by discounting the net cash flow in each period by the discount rate to the power of the time period and then adding these discounted cash flows over the horizon of the analysis. Table 5.1 organizes cash flows for each category by the time period used in the analysis (in this case, by year). Note that a more accurate NPV can be obtained using a shorter time period. Ultimately you could calculate NPV per second, but that is far too precise. Your savings account is probably calculated on a daily basis. For purposes of analysis, a monthly period is probably good. But the shorter the time period, the more spreadsheet rows would be required, and the harder it would be to display. We will use a year as our time horizon.

NPV is obtained by aggregating each time period's cash flow and dividing by the discount rate to the power of the time period, as shown in Table 5.2 using a discount rate of 1.1 per year.

Table 5.2. Net Present Value Calculation—Example Proposal

Year	Net cash flow	Discounted
1	−3,250,000	−2,954,545
2	+450,000	+41,322
3	+690,000	+518,407
4	+1,669,000	+1,139,949
5	+3,105,900	+1,928,520
Total	+2,264,900	+673,653

For Year 1, the total cash flow (benefits minus all five expense categories) is −$3,250,000. That is equivalent in today's value to −$3,250,000/(1.1^1), or $2,954,545. For Year 2, the total cash flow is +$50,000, equivalent in today's value to $50,000/(1.1^2), or $41,322. In this case, over the 5-year planning horizon, nominal net cash flow is estimated to be a net gain of over $2 million. This stream of cash flow at the cost of capital (discount rate) of 1.1 is a net gain of $673,653, indicating that at the cost of capital used, over the planning horizon considered, this is a worthwhile investment. (The indicator is whether or not the sum of discounted cash flows is positive or not.)

Note that if we increased the discount rate to 1.2, the NPV would be a negative $221,234, meaning that the proposal would not financially justify a cost of capital of 20% per year. This implies that the proposal would break even if the project achieved somewhere between a 10% and a 20% rate of return. We can try various discount rates on a spreadsheet until we identify a discount rate just above 16.9% where the NPV will be zero. The implication is that this investment would return 16.9% per year on the investment.

Cash flow analyses of this type are very useful, especially with spreadsheet support. It clearly displays the many assumptions made. It is common for business decision makers to be uncertain about most of the entries in the spreadsheet. In fact, it is common for different individuals to have different beliefs about specific assumed values. The good thing about spreadsheet analysis of expected cash flow is that each different set of assumptions could be entered, and expected NPV identified.

Payback

One of the most common reasons for company failure in the United States is lack of cash flow. In our example, if the firm has cash flow difficulties, the investment would be less attractive than if they had adequate cash reserves. Making the assumption that over time cash flow will turn positive at some point and remain positive thereafter, we can use another metric, payback, to identify the time until the investment will be recovered. This could be done in net present value terms (using discounted cash flows), or in nominal terms (with undiscounted cash flow). Either way, payback is interested in how long it will take to recover investment. The calculation is simply cumulative cash flow. Given the assumption of an initial investment leading to future positive cash flows, the time until cumulative cash flow turns positive is payback time. This is often used by decision makers to gauge the attractiveness of an investment. Table 5.3 shows calculations for our example SCM system, for both nominal and discounted cash flow.

Here the payback period is under 5 years in both cases. Using nominal (undiscounted) values, it would take 4 years and just over 3 months to recover the initial investment (assuming a linear rate of cash flow in year 5). With the discounted numbers, it would take 4 years and almost 8 months to recover the investment. In either case, the payback is between 4 and 5 years. We can also see that the firm will need cash reserves of at least $3,250,000 to survive the project (nearly $3 million in net present value terms).

Table 5.3. Payback Calculation

Year	Net (undiscounted)	Cumulative	Net (discounted 10%)	Cumulative
1	−3,250,000	−3,250,000	−2,954,545	−2,954,525
2	+50,000	−3,200,000	+41,322	−2,913,223
3	+690,000	−2,510,000	+518,407	−2,394,816
4	1,669,000	−841,000	+1,139,949	−1,254,866
5	+2,264,900	+1,928,520	+673,653	+673,653

Sensitivity Analysis

A very good thing about spreadsheet cash flow models is that you can include any assumption. (On the other hand, the bad thing is that so many assumptions are required!) To demonstrate, we might assume a vocal minority on the board thinks that the expected rate of benefit increase is too high, and instead of 30% growth in benefits after Year 2, they expect that these benefits will only grow at the rate of 10% annually. We can demonstrate the impact of this assumption change in Table 5.4. (That's what sensitivity analysis is—checking for the impact of changed entries into the model.)

Here the assumption in benefit growth in Years 4 and 5 doesn't change the decision if payback is desired within 5 years. But the project would be expected to be much less profitable (to the tune of $2 million in nominal cash flow). The NPV at 10% discount would drop to –$630,282, indicating that with the lower benefit growth assumption, the project would not return 10% per year. The return on investment (ROI) turns out to be 1.021, or an average of 2.1% return on the firm's money. They could probably find better things to do with their investment capital should benefit growth be the more conservative.

The problem with cash flow spreadsheet analysis is that practically every entry is an assumption, which could be debated. As we said, the nice thing is that it is easy to change and see the impact of any one assumption (or set of assumptions). But there can be many details to check.

Table 5.4. *Impact of Benefit Growth Rate*

Year	Expenses	High benefits	High cumulative	Low benefits	Low cumulative
1	3,250,000		−3,250,000		−3,250,000
2	2,000,000	2,000,000	−3,200,000	2,000,000	−3,200,000
3	3,000,000	3,000,000	−2,510,000	3,000,000	−2,510,000
4	3,900,000	3,900,000	−841,000	3,300,000	−1,441,000
5	5,070,000	+2,264,900	3,630,000	+224,900	+224,900
Totals	11,705,100	13,970,000		11,930,000	

Value Analysis

Peter Keen proposed value analysis as an alternative to cost-benefit analysis in the evaluation of proposed information system projects. These projects, clearly attractive to business firms, suffer in that their benefits are often heavily intangible. For instance, decision support systems are meant to provide decision makers with more complete information for decision making. But what is the exact dollar value of improved decision making? We all expect the success of firms to be closely tied to effective decision making, but better decision making cannot be rationally and accurately measured.[3]

Value analysis was presented as a way to separate the benefits measured in intangible terms from costs, which are expected to be more accurately measurable. Those tangible benefits as well as costs can be dealt with in net present terms, which would provide a price tag for proposed projects. The value of the benefits would be descriptive, with the intent of showing the decision makers accurate descriptions of what they were getting, along with the net present price. The decision would then be converted to a shopping decision. Many of us buy automobiles, despite the fact that the net present cost of owning an automobile is negative. Automobiles provide many intangible benefits, such as making the driver look very sporty, letting the driver speed over the countryside, and letting the driver transport those they would like to impress. The dollar value of these intangible benefits is a matter of willingness to pay, which can be identified in monetary terms by observing the purchasing behavior of individuals. This measurement requires some effort and is different for each individual.

Assume a firm is considering five different ways to implement some or all of an SCM (plus the alternative of doing nothing). The options, with estimated investments and benefits, are given in Table 5.5.

Table 5.5. Alternative System Implementation Options for Example ERP

Alternative	Investment	NPV
A–Full vendor ERP implementation, all modules	$15 million	$5 million
B–Vendor ERP, only FA, MM and SCM modules	$11 million	$7 million
C–Vendor, only SCM module	$8 million	$8 million
D–In-house development	$25 million	–$2 million
E–Open-sourced system	$3 million	$4 million
F–Do nothing (current system)	0	0

Table 5.6. Qualitative Features of ERP Options in Example

Alternative	BPR	Standardize	Internet	Advantage	Keep up	Disruption
A–Full	Complete	Complete	Best	Equal	Best	5 years
B–FA, MM, SCM	Partial	Partial	Best	Less than A	Less than A	4 years
C–SCM	Minimal	Partial	Best	Less than B	Less than B	1 year
D–In house	Complete	Complete	Problematic	Best	Mediocre	7 years
E–Open source	Minimal	Partial	Good	Moderate	Low	2 years
F–Nothing	Nothing	Nothing	Worst	Worst	Worst	0

Value analysis would consist of presenting the decision maker with the intangible comparisons in performance and placing the decision in the context of whether or not the decision maker thought the improvements provided by the new machine were worth their price tag. This requires an analysis of expected benefits from each system. The following are reasons this particular management team is interested in an SCM:

- To update current business processes (through business process reengineering)
- To standardize procedures within the organization
- To make interaction with suppliers and customers over web technology possible
- To gain strategic advantage
- To keep up with competitors
- To minimize system disruption
- To maximize positive net financial impact

The expected performance of each alternative on the six qualitative factors is given in Table 5.6.

In this approach, the expected benefits are understood to be highly variable and are treated as a rough estimate. Costs are assumed to be a bit more reliable. Thus the options, in descending order of price, are as follows:

A—Full implementation of vendor product expected to cost $15 million:

- Complete BPR analysis and standardization
- Top-of-the-line Internet access for suppliers and customers
- State-of-the-art ERP system, which competitors also have access to
- Serious disruption of operations through installation in 5 years

Expected benefit: NPV $20 million, for net gain of $5 million.

B—Partial implementation of vendor product expected to cost $11 million:

- Partial BPR analysis and standardization
- Top-of-the-line Internet access for suppliers and customers
- State-of-the-art for modules obtained, which competitors also have access to
- Serious disruption of operations through installation in 4 years

Expected benefit: NPV $18 million, for net gain of $7 million.

C—Minimal implementation of vendor product expected to cost $8 million:

- Minimal BPR analysis, partial standardization
- Top-of-the-line Internet access for suppliers and customers
- State-of-the-art for SCM only, which competitors also have access to
- Serious disruption of operations through installation in 1 year

Expected benefit: NPV $16 million, for net gain of $8 million.

D—In-house implementation expected to cost $25 million:

- Complete BPR analysis and standardization
- Suspect Internet access for suppliers and customers
- Custom-designed system with features competitors don't have, but no best practices
- Serious disruption of operations through installation in seven years

Expected benefit: NPV $23 million, for net gain of –$2 million.

E—Open-sourced system expected to cost $3 million:

- Minimal BPR analysis and standardization
- Basic Internet access for suppliers and customers
- Proven ERP, but with less functionality than others
- Minimal impact on operations

Expected benefit: NPV $7, for net gain of $4 million.

F—Do nothing, expected to cost $0:

- No BPR analysis and standardization
- Primitive Internet access for suppliers and customers
- No ERP or SCM system, in market where competitors do
- No disruption of operations

Expected benefit: NPV $0, for net gain of $0 million.

Management can now view each option as a market basket of benefits, each with its own price tag. In this case, the key difference is building the system in-house, adopting a variant of the vendor system, installing an open-source software system, or doing nothing. Building the system in-house clearly has many risks and involves the most out-of-pocket investment. Management might well discard that option unless they are very confident in their ability to develop complex software projects. The open-sourced option has attractive features but involves more uncertainties and doesn't provide the best BPR options. Among the vendor options, Option A has the best features on reengineering, standardization, and Internet connectivity. But it would involve 5 years of disruption, and call for a $15 million investment. Option B would save $4 million in investment with the same Internet access at only 4 years of disruption but would sacrifice a bit on BPR factors, standardization, relative competitive advantage, and keeping up with competitors. Management might feel that the gains in disruption are worth the sacrifices in BPR, standardization, competitive advantage, and competitiveness. For only an $8 million investment, Option C would involve sacrifice of even more BPR, strategic advantage, and competitiveness but would save 3 additional years of disruption. However, it may be paramount to obtain higher degrees of methods improvement through business process reengineering and standardization of business functions across the organization.

By focusing on the important features involved, management may be able to conclude that Option A, B, or C is preferable to the other options available.

Taking value analysis one more step, to quantify these intangible benefits in terms of value (not in terms of dollars) takes us to multiple criteria analysis.

Multiple Objective Analysis

Profit has long been viewed as the determining objective of a business. However, as society becomes more complex, and as the competitive environment develops, businesses are finding that they need to consider multiple objectives. While short-run profit remains important, long-run factors such as market maintenance, product quality, and development of productive capacity often conflict with measurable short-run profit.

Conflicts are inherent in most interesting decisions. In business, profit is a valuable concentration point for many decision makers because it has the apparent advantage of providing a measure of worth. Minimizing risk becomes a second dimension for decision making. Cash flow needs become important in some circumstances. Businesses need developed markets to survive. The impact of advertising expenditure is often very difficult to forecast. Yet decision makers must consider advertising impact. Capital replenishment is another decision factor, which requires consideration of trade-offs. The greatest short-run profit will normally be obtained by delaying reinvestment in capital equipment. Many U.S. companies have been known to cut back capital investment in order to appear reasonably profitable to investors. Labor policies can also have impact on long-range profit. In the short run, profit will generally be improved by holding the line on wage rates and risking a high labor turnover. Some costs are not obvious, however, in such a policy. First, in a high-turnover environment, training costs rise. The experience of the members of an organization can be one of its most valuable assets. Second, it is difficult for employees to maintain a positive attitude when their experience is that short-run profit is always placed ahead of employee welfare. And innovative ideas are probably best found from those people who are involved with the grassroots of an organization—the workforce.

This variety of objectives presents decision makers with the need to balance conflicting objectives in ERP option selection. We will present the simple multiattribute rating technique (SMART), an easy-to-use method to aid selection decisions with multiple objectives.

Multiple criteria analysis considers benefits on a variety of scales without directly converting them to some common scale such as dollars. Multiple criteria analysis (with its many variants) is not at all perfect. But it does provide a way to demonstrate to decision makers the relative positive and negative features of alternatives and gives a way to quantify the preferences of decision makers.[4]

Fit with business procedures was selected among the three most important criteria by about one-half of the respondents and was listed as the single most important criterion by over one-third. While ERP vendors have devoted a great deal of effort to making their packages match existing business processes, the importance of this criterion is based on the high cost and bother of configuring and implementing ERP systems. Selection of a vendor involved less variance among criteria. Product functionality and quality were the criteria most often reported to be important.

Perhaps the easiest application of multiple criteria analysis is the SMART analysis, which identifies the relative importance of criteria in terms of weights and measures the relative performance of each alternative on each criterion in terms of scores.[5] We will first explain scores.

Scores: Scores in SMART can be used to convert performances (subjective or objective) to a zero-to-one scale, where zero represents the worst acceptable performance level in the mind of the decision maker and one represents the ideal, or possibly the best performance desired. Note that these ratings are subjective, a function of individual preference. Scores for the criteria given in the value analysis example could be as in Table 5.7.

Table 5.7. Scores by Criteria for Each Option in Example

Option	BPR	Standard	Internet	Advantage	Competition	Disruption	Financial
A	1.0	1.0	1.0	0.7	1.0	0.1	0.85
B	0.9	0.7	1.0	0.5	0.8	0.3	0.90
C	0.6	0.7	1.0	0.2	0.6	0.9	0.95
D	1.0	1.0	0.6	1.0	0.1	0.0	0.0
E	0.6	0.7	0.8	0.6	0.4	0.8	0.7
F	0.0	0.0	0.0	0.0	0.0	1.0	0.2

Table 5.8. Worst and Best Measures by Criteria

Criteria	Worst measure	Best measure
Update systems (BPR)	Nothing	Complete
Standardize business processes	Nothing	Complete
Internet connectivity to suppliers and customers	None	Modern
Gain strategic advantage	Do nothing	Develop unique system
Keep up with competition	Do nothing	State-of-the-art vendor
Minimize disruption	7-year installation	Current system
Financial implications	Risk $25 mil, lose $2 mil	Risk $3 mil, gain $4 mil

Weights: The next phase of the analysis ties these ratings together into an overall value function by obtaining the relative weight of each criterion. In order to give the decision maker a reference about what exactly is being compared, the relative range between best and worst on each scale for each criterion should be explained. Many methods are available to determine these weights. In SMART, the process begins with rank-ordering the four criteria. A possible ranking for a specific decision maker might be as given in Table 5.8.

To obtain relative criterion weights, the first step is to rank-order criteria by importance. Two estimates of weights can be obtained. The first assigns the least important criterion 10 points and assesses the relative importance of each of the other criteria on that basis. This process (including rank-ordering and assigning relative values based on moving from worst measure to best measure based on most important criterion) is demonstrated in Tables 5.9 and 5.10.

Table 5.9. Weight Estimation From Perspective of Most Important Criterion

Criteria	Worst measure	Best measure	Assigned value
1-Gain strategic advantage	Do nothing	Develop unique system	100
2-Keep up with competition	Do nothing	Use state-of-the-art	70
3-Internet connectivity	None	Modern	50
4-Update systems (BPR)	Nothing	Complete	30
5-Minimize disruption	7-year installation	Current system	20
6-Financial implications	Risk $25 mil, lose $2 mil	Risk $3 mil, gain $4 mil	10
7-Standardize business processes	Nothing	Complete	3

Table 5.10. Weight Estimation From Perspective of Least Important Criterion

Criteria	Worst measure	Best measure	Assigned value
7-Standardize business processes	Nothing	Complete	10
6-Financial implications	Risk $25 mil, lose $2 mil	Risk $3 mil, gain $4 mil	25
5-Minimize disruption	7-year installation	Current system	30
4-Update systems (BPR)	Nothing	Complete	50
3-Internet connectivity	None	Modern	60
2-Keep up with competition	Do nothing	Use state-of-the-art	70
1-Gain strategic advantage	Do nothing	Develop unique system	100

The total of the assigned values in Table 5.9 is 283. One estimate of relative weights is obtained by dividing each assigned value by 283. Before we do that, we obtain a second estimate from the perspective of the least important criterion, which is assigned a value of 10 as in Table 5.10.

These assigned values in Table 5.10 add up to 345. The two weight estimates are now as shown in Table 5.11.

Table 5.11. Criterion Weight Development

Criteria	Based on best		Based on worst		Compromise
1-Gain strategic advantage	100/283	0.35	100/345	0.29	0.33
2-Keep up with competition	70/283	0.25	70/345	0.20	0.23
3-Internet connectivity	50/283	0.18	60/345	0.17	0.17
4-Update systems (BPR)	30/283	0.11	50/345	0.14	0.12
5-Minimize disruption	20/283	0.07	30/345	0.09	0.08
6-Financial implications	10/283	0.04	25/345	0.07	0.05
7-Standardize business processes	3/283	0.01	10/345	0.03	0.02

The last criterion can be used to make sure that the sum of compromise weights adds up to 1.00.

Value Score: The next step of the SMART method is to obtain value scores for each alternative by multiplying each score on each criterion for an alternative by that criterion's weight and adding these products by alternative. Table 5.12 shows this calculation.

These value scores (shown in the totals row) provide a relative score that can be used to select (take the alternative with the highest value score), or to rank-order (by value score). In this case, the SMART analysis indicates a preference for Option A, the full version of the vendor ERP system. This is followed relatively by Option B, which is to reduce functionality to finance and accounting and materials management modules. Other options have lower ratings, while doing nothing is practically off the chart in a negative way.

Table 5.12. Value Score Calculation

Criteria	Weight	Option A	Option B	Option C	Option D	Option E	Option F
Strategic advantage	0.33	× 0.7 = 0.231	× 0.5 = 0.165	× 0.2 = 0.066	× 1.0 = 0.330	× 0.6 = 0.198	× 0.0 = 0.000
Competition	0.23	× 1.0 = 0.230	× 0.8 = 0.184	× 0.6 = 0.138	× 0.1 = 0.023	× 0.4 = 0.092	× 0.0 = 0.000
Internet	0.17	× 1.0 = 0.170	× 1.0 = 0.170	× 1.0 = 0.170	× 0.6 = 0.102	× 0.8 = 0.136	× 0.0 = 0.000
Update (BPR)	0.12	× 1.0 = 0.120	× 0.9 = 0.108	× 0.6 = 0.072	× 1.0 = 0.120	× 0.6 = 0.072	× 0.0 = 0.000
Minimize disrupt	0.08	× 0.1 = 0.008	× 0.3 = 0.024	× 0.9 = 0.072	× 0.0 = 0.000	× 0.8 = 0.064	× 1.0 = 0.080
Financial	0.05	× 0.85 = 0.043	× 0.9 = 0.045	× 0.95 = 0.048	× 0.0 = 0.000	× 0.7 = 0.035	× 0.20 = 0.010
Standardize	0.02	× 1.0 = 0.020	× 0.7 = 0.014	× 0.7 = 0.014	× 1.0 = 0.020	× 0.7 = 0.014	× 0.0 = 0.000
Totals	1.00	0.822*	0.710	0.580	0.595	0.611	0.090

Supply Chain Software ERP Issues

Supply chain software can be very effective in managing large supply chains. Unfortunately, more than 90% of the companies that have implemented ERP systems have not had a truly successful implementation the first time around.[6]

- Supply chain software should be motivated by accurate strategic and tactical process improvement objectives, with documented assumptions and valid ROI expectations and metrics.
- Supply chain software must be implemented appropriately and in a timely manner to attain ROI expectations.

These two points may seem obvious, but supply chain management is not usually initially approached in this manner. As a result, many problems come to pass during and after implementation. This often requires a reimplementation effort or at least a major tune-up. ROI comes from process improvements that supply chain software supports, not from new software itself. What's the difference? Software alone, no matter how good it is, has little impact on improving business performance. If you continue to use presoftware business processes after implementation, you can anticipate identical or possibly worse performance. Software can, on the other hand, enable many new processes.

ERP System Evaluation by Toroid International Ltd.

Adapted from H. S. C. Perera and W. K. R. Costa (2008), *The Journal of Business Perspective 12*(4).[7]

Toroid International is a transformer manufacturer with roughly 2,000 employees in Sri Lanka. They adopted an ERP system, based on the decision of top- and mid-level management advised by their information technology department. The original decision was based on Toroid's business strategy, mainly driven by cost. A detailed analysis of impact on the company was not conducted. Options considered were IFS, SAP, and Syteline ERP software packages. The original decision was supported primarily by vendor recommendations.

Perera and Costa proposed a multiple criteria analysis for ERP system selection, suing the Toroid case history to demonstrate the use of analytic hierarchy process (AHP) in this context. Judgments were based on input from the three top managers who had participated in the ERP implementation. Criteria considered were as follows:

- Business strategy
- Improved supply chain management
- Increased customer support
- Decreased risk
- Functional fit
- Technology
- Vendor position
- Cost and benefits
- Management changes

AHP was used to generate weights for the seven major criteria (the weight for business strategy split into 0.75 for supply chain management aspects and 0.25 for increasing customer support). AHP was also used to score each of the three candidate packages on these seven criteria. Evaluation was conducted using Expert Choice software. Table 5.13 gives resulting scores and weights.

Table 5.13. Toroid International ERP Selection Data

Criteria	Weight	SAP score	IFS score	Syteline score
Business strategy	0.323	0.327	0.369	0.304
Change management	0.040	0.311	0.266	0.423
Risk	0.040	0.250	0.416	0.334
Functional fit	0.149	0.360	0.345	0.295
Cost and benefits	0.288	0.271	0.135	0.594
Technology	0.063	0.333	0.333	0.333
Vendor position	0.097	0.409	0.305	0.285
Overall score		0.320	0.287	0.392

The study confirmed the decision that Toroid had made, with the adopted Syteline system receiving the highest score. Table 5.13 demonstrates that Syteline's greatest advantage was in cost and benefits, which had a relatively high weight.

Conclusion

Many costs arise when implementing supply chain software. Many of these are hidden and especially difficult to estimate because most organizations don't repeat the exercise. We have reviewed some of the primary methods used to evaluate SCM proposals. Cost-benefit analysis (with net present value used if the time dimension is present) is the ideal approach from the theoretical perspective but has a number of limitations. It is very difficult to measure benefits and also difficult to measure some aspects of costs accurately. One view of dealing with this problem is to measure more accurately. Economists have developed ways to estimate the value of a life and the value of scenic beauty. However, these measures are difficult to sell to everybody.

Cost-benefit analysis provides an ideal way to proceed if there are no intangible factors (or at least no important intangible factors). However, usually such factors are present. Intermediate approaches, such as payback analysis and value analysis, exist to deal with some cases. More complex cases are better supported by multiple criteria analysis. One of the most obvious difficulties is that benefits, and even costs, can involve high levels of uncertainty. The element of chance can be included in cost-benefit calculations by using Monte Carlo simulation.[8]

Value analysis is one such alternative method. Value analysis isolates intangible benefits from those benefits and costs that are more accurately measurable in monetary terms and relies on decision-maker judgment to come to a more informed decision. The SMART method, one of a family of multiple criteria decision analysis techniques, provides a way to quantify these intangible factors to allow decision makers to trade off values.

CHAPTER 6

Supply Chain Software Installation Project Management

Supply chain management support can be obtained many ways, some of which were discussed in chapter 5. Regardless of how a supply chain management (SCM) system is acquired, installing it is a major project. Project plans need to be aggressive, because SCM systems are very critical to organizational efficiency (the sooner the system is brought online, the sooner benefits are obtained). It is difficult to reliably estimate durations of any information systems project. Due to the need to balance realism with urgency, schedules should be aggressive but achievable.

The type of SCM system adopted will impact the need for changes. Adoption of a single vendor package without modifications will reduce the need for customization, and thus will reduce project complexity, which fosters better schedule performance. However, the primary objective is to develop the right system for the organization. Implementing the enterprise resource planning (ERP) system on time and on budget is important, but it is more important to implement the right ERP system.

A project management steering committee is very important to ERP implementation project success. This committee should include senior management representing affected corporate functions, as well as representative end users. This committee usually is involved in system selection, as well as monitoring project progress and management of external consultants. Consultants provide experience missing from the organization and can be invaluable. However, consultants should be screened to avoid those with financial ties to software vendors and lack of experience in the specific system being implemented.

Perhaps the single most decisive element of SCM installation success or failure is the knowledge, skills, abilities, and experience of the project manager. An SCM installation project manager must understand both the business and the technology. Private and public sector organizations are increasing their use of enterprise information systems (EISs), which make integrated financial and human resources solutions available that facilitate public sector business processes. While procuring the right EIS system is an important factor, the genuine challenge lies in implementing these systems, which can be tremendously complex. Today's EIS project managers are faced with overwhelming challenges. As government and private system users' budgets have become leaner, project managers have to achieve more with less in tighter time frames. This chapter addresses the explicit needs of the private/public-sector EIS project manager, with wide-ranging know-how in private/public-sector project management.

Project management is one of the most important fields in information systems. It is difficult to bring an information systems project to completion on time, within budget, and meeting specifications. Reports issued by the Standish Group based on surveys of IT companies repeatedly find that only about 15% come in on time and within budget. For large companies, the success rate is lower. While EIS systems involve a little more structure than the average IT project, there still are problems encountered in implementing EIS. A typical problem is underestimation of the time to get an EIS system working. However, there have been a number of efforts to make this type of installation less problematic. One major reason is that vendors have a vested interest in making EIS installation less risky and more predictable.

Implementation Process

Three broad approaches to the timing and location of EIS implementation include the pilot implementation approach, the Big Bang implementation approach, and the phased implementation approach:

- *Pilot implementation approach*—This approach starts with a small-scale version applied to a small division or with one specific module, such as finance and accounting, with the intent of seeing how that initial effort works before jeopardizing the rest of the organization. The thought is to prioritize the functional areas and to bring into operation that area offering the greatest advantage first. This requires an enormous amount of interface programming to preserve the data flows between the legacy system and the new module being implemented. It is also the lowest risk alternative but also takes the most time as each module is rolled out.

- *Big Bang implementation approach*—This requires simultaneous implementation of multiple modules of an EIS package at one time. Why is it called Big Bang? An organization prepares, tests, trains, and everything else needed to get ready, and then over a weekend or a few days the data in the old system is migrated to the new one. One morning everyone in the company starts using the new system and the old one is simultaneously turned off. This is the most risky alternative. There will always be unforeseen and unexpected events. Several famous companies have been caught in this trap. Usually high technology companies that thought it could not happen to them found that it could. A variant of the Big Bang approach is to combine it with a phased approach. This entails a series of "minibangs" that affect a logical segment of the business. One example uses a division-by-division approach where each one uses a Big Bang to migrate to the new ERP system. A second example might use a functional approach, on the other hand this requires interfaces with both systems running their parts of the company, that is, finance goes first with the new system implemented in all divisions at one time, followed by manufacturing and customer support.
- *Phased implementation approach*—consists of designing, developing, testing, and installing different modules of the EIS over time or rolled over different elements of the organization at different times.

Implementation Issues

ERP solutions ultimately help in ensuring that data is transparently available across the enterprise. The advantages of implementing a good ERP system are manifold. With its integrated applications, an ERP system optimizes the core processes of an organization, accelerates transactions with its business workflow, and makes strategic management information available in a transparent form at all levels of the company, within the framework of its information warehouse concept. An ERP system guarantees strategic freedom in designing an organization's information management communication. This enables uniformity in storage and restricted exchange of business data between two physically divided application systems. Ready-to-wear solutions for more than a few hundred business processes are available in an ERP solution that can be promptly constructed using its business process such as modeling tools to optimize the processes of an organization. With its business-oriented functions, an ERP solution opens up new opportunities for improving an organization's market and customer orientation through data mining techniques. The high level of flexibility is easy to get through ERP systems and enables the flexibility to respond to a continually changing market situation.

Where vendor software installation money is spent is of interest. In the ERP field, two surveys[1] in manufacturing industries found the results shown in Table 6.1.

In the United States, vendors seem to take the biggest chunk of the average implementation. Consultants also take a big portion. These proportions are reversed in Sweden. The internal implementation team accounts for an additional 14% (12% in Sweden). These proportions are roughly reversed in Sweden with training.

Table 6.1. EIS Installation Project Cost Proportions

Installation cost proportion	United States	Sweden
Software	30%	24%
Consulting	24%	30%
Hardware	18%	19%
Implementation team	14%	12%
Training	11%	14%
Other	3%	1%

Source: Extracted from Mabert et al. (2000); Olhager and Selldin (2003).

ERP/SCM Installation Project Risk

Managing risk on an EIS project is crucial to its success. A risk is a potential failure point. An EIS project may have thousands, maybe even millions, of potential failure points, in the form of untested technology (and untested staff), political events, and even nature. When computers interact with how humans do their jobs, often unintended consequences occur. We can broadly categorize steps to manage risk:

1. Find potential failure points or risks.
2. Analyze the potential failure points to determine the damage they might do.
3. Assess the probability of the failure occurring.
4. Based on the first three factors, prioritize the risks.
5. Mitigate the risks through whatever action is necessary.

Project team members must rely on their experience and advice from others to find potential failure points or risks. Track through the entire project plan and look for areas of ambiguity:

Step 1: One of the easiest and most effective ways to find potential failure points is to talk to other organizations that have done the same projects. Cost estimates are probably the most common potential project failure point. Other potential failure points include lack of an executive sponsor, an under qualified project manager, and no clear objectives for the project.

Step 2: The next step is to determine the severity of the potential failure on the budget, project timeline, or the users' requirements.

Step 3: Assessing the likely impact and the probability of the failure occurring is more art than science, requiring in-depth knowledge of both the EIS package and the business. A risk management team should be built that brings together those individuals that have the knowledge and experience to know what might happen. This team must have experience in implementing the specific EIS package for an organization approximately the same size and in the same industry as yours.

Step 4: Based on the first two factors, prioritize risks. Decide which risks should be eliminated completely, because of potential for heavy impact on critical business processes. Set up a monitoring plan for risks that should have regular management attention. Make the entire team aware of those risks.

Step 5: You mitigate risks by reducing either the probability or the impact. The probability can be reduced by action up front to ensure that a particular risk is reduced. The project risk plan should include a set of steps to recover from each risk, should failure occur. The team must know the person accountable for recovery from each specific risk, and the action to be taken to resolve it. The team must know the symptoms of the impending failure, and act to prevent it from occurring if possible. An example is to test a particular operating system or hardware component to prove that it works prior to going live. Doing a pilot implementation or prototyping the first set of EIS interfaces are both examples of risk mitigation.

Project Management

To demonstrate the relative aspects of installing various forms of ERP/SCM, we will start with a simple critical path model (CPM) representing selection of the SCM variant for an organization. Microsoft Project uses the traditional CPM, which consists of a list of project activities, each of these activity's duration, and immediate predecessors. Microsoft Project allows extending project management to resources required. Inputs are given in Table 6.2.

This is a fairly straightforward sequence of activities, which can be graphically displayed in a network, as shown in Figure 6.1. Networks also provide a valuable visual aid for managers to identify relationships among activities.

The sequence of events here is clear—activities B and C can work in parallel once activity A is accomplished. All other activities are sequential—they can't begin until their predecessors are finished. A predecessor relationship is captured by the critical path method. In reality, these relationships are often not as rigid as the critical path method

Table 6.2. Activity List for Full EIS System

Activity	Duration	Result
A–Select consultant for selecting system	2 weeks	none
B–Meet with consultant to discuss ERP	4 weeks	A
C–Meet with Board of Directors to explain proposal	1 week	A
D–Develop request for proposals to give to vendors	3 weeks	B, C
E–Obtain vendor proposals	4 weeks	D
F–Develop organization business cases including training	8 weeks	E
G–Present business cases to Board of Directors	1 week	F
H–Redo estimates in light of board requests for changes	3 weeks	G
I–Initiate installation project	1 week	H

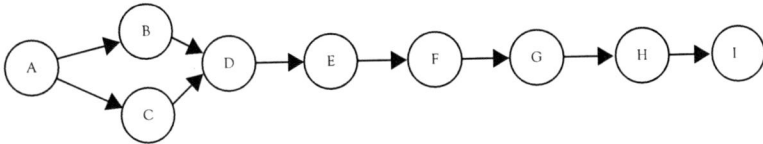

Figure 6.1. Network for ERP system selection scenario.

assumes. For instance, analysts could anticipate and begin work on activity D before the board approved the concept. Such an early start would run the risk of wasting time if the board were to disapprove the proposal. But if management considered this to be of low likelihood, and if the benefit of getting a jump start on estimation seemed worth the risk, modifications to the implied set of precedence relationships could be made. It is necessary to understand specifically what the critical path method assumes in order to make use of its output.

Another graphical outcome of the critical path method is a *Gantt chart*, which displays the early start schedule versus time (Figure 6.2). A *schedule* can be generated over a period of weeks based on the *early start* implied for all activities.

Figure 6.2 gives the Microsoft Project Gantt chart for this project. A Gantt chart shows the time periods when each activity is scheduled to occur. The critical paths (project activities that must be completed on time if the overall project is to finish on time) are identified by a color.

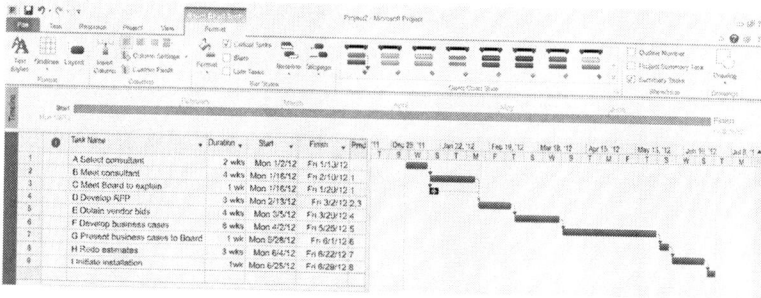

Figure 6.2. Schedule for ERP system selection scenario.

If everything went according to plan, this project would be completed in 26 weeks. The activity list, estimated durations, and predecessor relationships are all the information items required to develop a critical path model. That also means that all other information like uncertain durations and limited resources are assumed away in the critical path method. The initial step of the critical path method is to generate the early start schedule.

Early Start Schedule: For every activity that has no unscheduled predecessors, schedule the activity to start as soon as possible (either the project start time—usually time 0 for reference—or the maximum early finish of all predecessors). The critical path schedules are optimal with respect to time. This process continues until all activities are scheduled. The early finish is the sum of the early start time plus the duration as shown in Table 6.3:

Table 6.3. Early Start Schedule for ERP System Selection Scenario

Activity	Duration	Predecessors	Early start	Early finish	Result
A	2 weeks	none	0	2	Releases B, C
B	4 weeks	A	2	6	Releases D
C	1 week	A	2	3	Must be done to start D
D	3 weeks	B,C	6	9	Releases E
E	4 weeks	D	9	13	Releases F
F	8 weeks	E	13	21	Releases G
G	1 week	F	21	22	Releases H
H	3 weeks	G	22	25	Releases I
I	1 week	H	25	26	Finishes project

Late Start Schedule: The next phase of the critical path analysis is the late start schedule. The late start schedule is the latest an activity can be scheduled without delaying project completion time. The final ending time for the project can be some contract deadline, which may be different from the early finish schedule, or the early finish project completion time can be used. If the deadline is earlier than the project early finish time, the project is infeasible (can't be completed on time with given durations). If the deadline is later than the project early finish time, all activities in the project will have slack or spare time. If the deadline coincides with the project early finish time, there will be at least one *critical path*, connecting activities in a chain with zero slack.

The late start schedule is calculated in reverse. Networks are not really needed for development of early start schedules but are very useful in sorting out the relationships for late start schedules. Begin with the end time (deadline or early finish time). All activities that do not appear on the list of predecessors for unscheduled activities can be scheduled. The late finish time will be either the project end time or the minimum of the late start times for all following activities. While networks usually aren't required to do an early start schedule, they can be handy in sorting out the abstraction involved in working backwards during development of the late start schedule. The late start schedule for our scenario is shown in Table 6.4.

Table 6.4. Late Start Schedule for ERP System Selection Scenario

Activity	Duration	Followers	Early finish	Early start	Result
I	1 week	None	26	25	Releases H
H	3 weeks	I	25	22	Releases G
G	1 week	H	22	21	Releases F
F	8 weeks	G	21	13	Releases E
E	4 weeks	D	13	9	Releases D
D	3 weeks	E	9	6	Releases B, C
C	1 week	D	6	2	Releases A
B	4 weeks	D	6	2	Must be started before A can finish
A	2 weeks	B,C	2	0	Late start schedule done

Here the only case where there were multiple early starts to compare was for activity A. Activity A's early finish was the minimum of the early start for all activities that were followers of activity A (in this case activities B and C). The minimum early start for those two activities was 2, so the earliest A could finish without delaying the overall project would be the end of Week 2.

Slack is the difference between the late start and early start schedules (it doesn't matter which you use, because in both cases the difference between start and finish is the duration). Those activities with zero slack are critical. If they are delayed, the project completion time would be delayed. There can be more than one critical path for a project, and the project network presented in Figure 6.1 can be useful in ensuring identification of each critical path. Table 6.5 shows identification of slack.

Slack in the case exists for only one activity, C. One critical path of activities, consisting of the chain of activities from A to I, has zero slack. More complex projects will include slack for multiple activities.

CPM Models of Supply Chain Software Options

In chapter 5, we considered a variety of means to obtain supply chain software. The first option was to install a complete EIS vendor system, including an SCM module. Table 6.6 gives a general list of activities, some of which might not be used by particular options, but which serve as a general installation project framework. Durations would depend on

Table 6.5. Calculation of Slack for ERP Project Selection Scenario

Activity	Early start	Early finish	Late start	Late finish	Slack	Critical?
A	0	2	0	2	0	Yes
B	2	6	2	6	0	Yes
C	2	3	5	6	3	No
D	6	9	6	9	0	Yes
E	9	13	9	13	0	Yes
F	13	21	13	21	0	Yes
G	21	22	21	22	0	Yes
H	22	25	22	25	0	Yes
I	25	26	25	26	0	Yes

Table 6.6. Activity List for Supply Chain Software Installation

Activity	Duration	Predecessors
1. Meet with consultant		none
2. Obtain vendor (provider) proposals		1
3. Business case		2
4. Obtain board approval	0	3
5. Form internal team	2 weeks	4
6. BPR		4
7. Develop sandbox		4
8. Train superusers		7
9. Set vendor software parameters		6
10. Phase 1 Installation		5,9
11. Phase 1 Testing		10
12. Phase 1 Load data		11
13. Phase 1 Go live	0	12
14. Phase 2 Installation		13
15. Phase 2 Testing		14
16. Phase 2 Load data		15
17. Phase 2 Go live	0	16
18. Phase 3 Installation		17
19. Phase 3 Testing		18
20. Phase 3 Load data		19
21. Phase 3 Go live	0	20
22. Phase 1 Train users		8, 11
23. Phase 2 Train users		8, 15
24. Phase 3 Train users		8, 19

the option selected. Milestone activities all have zero durations. Forming the internal team would take 2 weeks regardless of which option was selected. All other durations vary by the specific option.

Duration data in Table 6.7 roughly demonstrate time differences in the options discussed. Developing an in-house or open-source system involves more internal development.

Activity 4 is an example of a *milestone*, an activity with zero duration. This is an event, in this case triggering the development of an employee training program for an organization adopting the system. The network for this project is given in Figure 6.3.

Table 6.7. *Activity Durations by Option*

Activity	Full ERP vendor system	3-module vendor system	SCM only	In-house	Open source	ASP
1. Meet with consultant	1 week	1 week	1 week			
2. Obtain proposals	4 weeks	4 weeks	4 weeks			1 week
3. Business case	10 weeks	8 weeks	5 weeks	10 weeks	5 weeks	5 weeks
4. Obtain board approval	0	0	0	0	0	0
5. Form internal team	2 weeks	2 weeks	2 weeks	2 weeks	2 weeks	2 weeks
6. BPR	12 weeks	9 weeks	5 weeks	15 weeks	8 weeks	
7. Develop sandbox	5 weeks	4 weeks	2 weeks	3 weeks	2 weeks	5 weeks
8. Train superusers	6 weeks	5 weeks	4 weeks	1 week	3 weeks	6 weeks
9. Set vendor parameters	15 weeks	12 weeks	6 weeks			1 week
25. Development				26 weeks	5 weeks	
10. Phase 1 Installation	3 weeks	2 weeks	1 weeks	6 week	2 weeks	1 week
11. Phase 1 Testing	4 weeks	3 weeks	2 weeks	12 weeks	5 weeks	1 week
12. Phase 1 Load data	3 weeks	2 weeks	2 weeks	2 weeks	3 weeks	3 weeks
13. Phase 1 Go live	0	0	0	0	0	0
14. Phase 2 Installation	3 weeks	2 weeks				
15. Phase 2 Testing	4 weeks	3 weeks				
16. Phase 2 Load data	3 weeks	2 weeks				
17. Phase 2 Go live	0	0				
18. Phase 3 Installation	3 weeks					
19. Phase 3 Testing	4 weeks					
20. Phase 3 Load data	3 weeks					
21. Phase 3 Go live	0					
22. Phase 1 Train users	3 weeks	3 weeks	3 weeks	1 week	3 weeks	3 weeks
23. Phase 2 Train users	3 weeks	3 weeks				
24. Phase 3 Train users	3 weeks					

The Gantt chart from Microsoft Project for the full vendor system with three phases is given in Figure 6.4, with the critical path displayed in red in Microsoft Project (dark gray in Figure 6.4).

Project slack is displayed with bars for noncritical activities. These slacks can be calculated in Excel as shown in Table 6.8.

In this case, one critical path consists of activities 1 to 6, 9 to 13, and

Table 6.8. Calculation of Slack for SCM Only System

Activity	Duration	Early start	Early finish	Late start	Late finish	Slack	Critical?
1. Meet with consultant	1	0	1	0	1	0	Yes
2. Obtain proposals	4	1	5	1	5	0	Yes
3. Business case	5	5	10	5	10	0	Yes
4. Obtain board approval	0	10	10	10	10	0	Yes
5. Form internal team	2	10	12	19	21	9	No
6. BPR	5	10	15	10	15	0	Yes
7. Develop sandbox	2	10	12	20	22	10	No
8. Train superusers	4	12	16	22	26	10	No
9. Set vendor parameters	6	15	21	15	21	0	Yes
10. Phase 1 installation	1	21	22	21	22	0	Yes
11. Phase 1 testing	2	22	24	22	24	0	Yes
12. Phase 1 load data	2	24	26	24	26	0	Yes
13. Phase 1 go live	0	26	26	26	26	0	Yes
22. Phase 1 train users	3	26	29	26	29	0	Yes

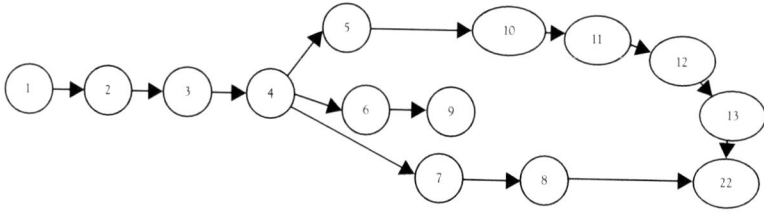

Figure 6.3. Network for framework with one phase.

22. It is possible to have parallel sets of critical activities in more than one path. Looking at the list of critical activities will not automatically identify the critical path. This list needs to be considered in light of the network. Shared slack and independent slack are the two kinds of slack. *Shared slack* is slack that is shared across more than one activity. For instance, both Activities 7 and 8 have 10 weeks of slack. This implies that some spare time is available in the accomplishment of these activities. However, if a week of delay were encountered in Activity 7, this would reduce the time available for Activity 8 as well. That is because it is the same 10 weeks of spare time in this case. Activity 5 has 9 weeks of *independent slack*.

Schonberger recommended focusing on scheduling the critical chain of activities closely, to make sure that they have the resources needed to proceed as scheduled.[2] Goldratt adopted the same view.[3] The critical chain of activities includes those activities that are critical (as long as managerial control can influence their duration) but is not limited to these activities. Activities with very little slack can become problems if they are delayed up to or beyond their slack. Therefore, the slack of noncritical activities should also be monitored, to make sure that new critical activities are identified.

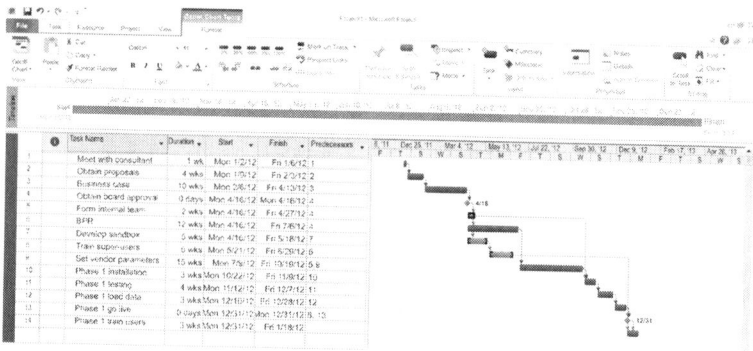

Figure 6.4. Microsoft Project display for partial vendor (1-phase) system.

We ran Microsoft Project models for each of the six systems. Comparative results are shown in Table 6.9.

Table 6.9 demonstrates a bit of the trade-off among different systems. More complex systems obviously are going to require longer installation projects. ASP projects are probably going to be the fastest to install. In-house systems can usually be expected to take the longest, although here our numbers show the full vendor ERP to take slightly longer, due to predecessor relationships imposed on the phases. There will be far greater duration uncertainty in the in-house and open-source options.

Projects have a bias in that activity delays accumulate, but any activities that finish early have to wait on other (slower) activities.[4] This is because when an activity is late, those that must wait for it to be completed start later than scheduled. On the other hand, if an activity should be finished before it was scheduled to finish, the advantage rarely can be used, because in complicated projects different crews and materials have to be gathered, and many different people need to be coordinated. The early finish time is not usually known much prior to the activity's completion. Therefore, it is very difficult to gather all the following activities' resources together in time to start early.

The following case demonstrates some of the difficulties encountered in implementing software projects within organizations.

Table 6.9. Supply Chain Software Alternative Model Results

	Slack—Form internal team	Slack—Develop sandbox/train	Finish date	Duration
Full ERP vendor system	25 weeks	26 weeks	6/7/2013	75 weeks
3-module vendor system	19 weeks	19 weeks	12/21/2012	51 weeks
SCM only	9 weeks	10 weeks	7/20/2012	29 weeks
In-house	60 weeks	57 weeks	5/17/2013	72 weeks
Open source	24 weeks	18 weeks	8/3/2012	31 weeks
ASP	12 weeks	0	5/18/2012	20 weeks

ERP Project Problems in Nevada DMV

The Nevada Department of Motor Vehicles (DMV), like most such organizations across the United States, sought to increase the efficiency of their service to taxpayers through automation. Nevada has been the fastest growing U.S. state in population for 15 consecutive years, reaching almost 2 million people (about 1.7 million of them in Las Vegas) by 2000. Nevada's DMV employed about 2,200 people in 36 offices in 1999, responsible to enforce statutes relating to motor vehicles and watercraft.

In 1999, the DMV handled over 130,000 vehicle registration renewals and 10,000 new vehicle registrations per month, in addition to 30,000 license renewals and 6,000 new driver licenses per month. The length of time customers had to wait was noticeably increasing. The DMV sought to improve cost, speed, and service quality.

The Nevada DMV adopted Project Genesis in 1996, a 7-year upgrade of 20-year old legacy computer systems. These legacy systems were altered and patched with the intent of dealing with the exploding workload, but they were unable to keep up. Separate systems handled registration and titles and driver's license information. This led to the need for multiple updating, and often customer information was not current, even though citizens had just updated data on one of the systems. There often were computer crashes, and technicians were not trained to work on both systems, meaning that citizens requiring service in both systems entered a second line as soon as their wait in the first line was over. Expected benefits were reduction in new hiring and improved customer service.

The project cost the Nevada DMV $34 million, completed in 2003. The system initially went online September 7, 1999. The first phase of the project included system development, continuous improvement, organizational change, and change management. A detailed plan of integration was generated, and vendor products explored. The second phase built on the first phase with the intent of providing one-stop service. The output of Phase 2 was a core system, with kiosks to give citizens information about driver's license, registration, and title requirements. A phone-processing center was created to answer citizen calls. Phase 3 continued the process by adding digital document imaging, online and telephone registration, and renewals by outside vendors.

The project was initially scheduled to go live in July 1999. In October 1998, all 500 DMV technicians were trained on the new processes. Two employees from each DMV were sent to extensive training of 6 months on the new system, while the rest of the technicians received an 8-hour course. This training continued through August 1999.

Conversion was expected to take 3 days and was to be done on a 3-day holiday weekend. As the launch date neared, it was delayed until early September due to unresolved bugs. This led to forcing out the DMV deputy director and heavy press and politician interest. There were still bugs in early September, but the governor insisted on going live.

The premature implementation was a disaster. Employees did not know how to use the system, and customer waiting time increased to hours. The DMV reverted to the old system (decided by the new deputy director) on September 7. The state legislature subcommittee in charge met in early October, agreeing that the new system had too many bugs. But the governor stated that abandoning Project Genesis was not an option. He announced a remedy plan involving hiring 42 new workers, 24-hour shifts to catch up with mail-in registration backlog, a 30-day grace period for police tickets for registration or license renewals, a telephone hotline, and Internet and telephone technology for registration. These steps were to be implemented by June 2000.

In November, average wait times in Las Vegas were reduced to around 2.5 hours (in the old system this transaction took 4 minutes, under Project Genesis this service time increased to 15 minutes).

The Genesis Project had been authorized by a legislative appropriation of $17.8 million in 1997. This was increased by $8.3 million in 1999. By October 1999, $25 million had been spent. By November 2002, DMV officials claimed that they had not exceeded their budget. However, these costs did not include impact on citizens.

This project seems to be quite typical. Implementation encountered a great deal of difficulty because a great deal of new programming and system installation needed to be accomplished, making these projects highly difficult to estimate in terms of time (and that impacts money). Typically cost overruns occur, although IT personnel usually find a way to justify some statement to the effect that they are within budget.

Source: Adapted from Dhillon and Caldeira (2008).

Conclusion

Proper planning and management is very important in supply chain management software implementation. Project management in the implementation of such software includes requirements to accomplish the following:

a. Software and hardware selection
b. Business process reengineering to gain effective advantage from the new system
c. Assessment of the ERP or SCM readiness of the organization and plan change management to make the new system effective

Proper project management includes the selection of an effective project management team. Implementing an EIS is not an inconsequential effort. Considerable attention should be given to the preliminary stages of planning. User requirements and selected functionality should be communicated to all involved in the project. Critical success factors need to be considered to carefully coordinate the efforts of the many people involved, to include consultants and managers. Gaining employee commitment to the EIS project is very important. Because the EIS integrates diverse company elements and data from many departments, the effects of delays ripple with dramatic impact. Therefore, control of the EIS implementation project is paramount.

CHAPTER 7

Recapitulation

This concluding chapter discusses three issues related to current events in enterprise systems. We want to emphasize the importance of training in obtaining effective use of enterprise resource planning (ERP) systems, supply chain management (SCM), advance planning systems (APSs), or electronic information systems (EISs). ERP systems have been around long enough and have had sufficient research leading to improved systems that upgrades have become important. This creates great pressure on organizations that perhaps spent billions on massive systems in the 1990s, now finding that vendors are suggesting they go through another round of massive installation and retraining with significant capital requirements. Upgrades are encouraged by vendors through dropping service on their older systems. (SAP announced around 2004 that they were discontinuing service on their flagship R3 system as of 2007. This was followed by client outcries, resulting in postponement of discontinued service until 2011.) A final topic is the evolution of added functionality. In the past, systems such as APS or customer relationship management (CRM) were added to ERP systems, with software provided by external vendors. This was changed when Oracle purchased Siebel Systems, the leading CRM vendor around 2005. Oracle thus made CRM a module within their ERP. SAP responded by purchasing their own CRM to make into a module. The same was done with SCM systems, to include APSs.

Training

In any supply chain software implementation, it is generally understood that training is a key component of organizational change management and of the overall success of the implementation. Many important issues remain in making SCM systems work. User training has shown up as a critical success factor in the implementation of an ERP in many studies.[1]

Managers often underestimate the magnitude required in such a training program. Training is typically underestimated and is often the first target for budget cutting. A period of about 1 year is usually required until the trauma of new system implementation passes. This difficult period is easier to cope with if a good, thorough training program is adopted. Furthermore, those organizations that do a poor job of training have been found to have poorer performing enterprise systems.[2]

Good training programs can pay off in many ways. Gartner has claimed that each hour of effective training is worth 5 hours to the organization because well-trained users take less than a quarter of the time to reach productive performance levels, they require less assistance from help sources, and they spend less time correcting errors.

Thus SCM training programs focus on transactional training (how the system works). SCM software companies and implementation teams are normally very good at delivering training that teaches employees how to accomplish transactions in the system. On the other hand, running a business entails much more than simply implementation transactions within a software program. SCM training programs should spotlight on new business processes.

Training Problems

EIS software itself is rarely the source of implementation problems. Poor training of users is usually the source of most implementation problems. Organizations with higher proportions of new employees may find implementation of EIS easier. Firms with many employees with many years of experience within the firm prior to EIS implementation require greater levels of change. Conversely, managerial and professional employees are often easier to convince of the positive impact of EIS on organizational effectiveness. Further, the degree of change required within the organization can have an impact on EIS installation timing. If the system is implemented too quickly, this may not provide sufficient time for the organizational climate to change.

Rarely do EIS implementations run smoothly. The following are some of the pitfalls organizations typically face:

- Placing employees in software-specific training, without attention to business processes
- Focusing training on command sequences without explanation of why skimping on training time
- Continuing tendency of new users to solve problems the old way rather than learn the new system

Training Media

A number of tools are available to deliver user training. One-way channels included newsletters, road shows, town meetings, a website, and personal appearances by key leaders to inform employees of what was developing in their IT. Interactive communication included workshops, meetings to deal with specific issues, conference calls, and collaboration websites. Hands-on interaction was also developed, to include *sandboxes* enabling users to play with the system using simulated data prior to using the real system.

Some of the reasons training in new EIS systems is difficult include user diversity, the complexity of the new system, and the variety of training methods available. By their nature, EIS systems are going to radically change how many people do their jobs. The theory of EIS is to integrate computer support to all aspects of the business, naturally leading to user diversity. These people also are busy, especially in coping with the requirements of the new system. Training users in new EIS systems can be extremely expensive, usually over 10% of total EIS system cost.

The need for flexibility in timing and place as well as the need for training in specific functions rather than the comprehensive EIS system have made it important to have flexible training delivery means. This has led to an entire industry providing EIS training. Many delivery formats are available, including the following:

- Web-based virtual training
- Computer-based training
- Video courses
- Self-study books
- Training manuals
- Pop-up help screens
- Classroom training

- Sandboxes, or prototype systems using simulated data for hands-on orientation

Enterprise system training should be conducted during business hours to indicate its importance.[3] V. Vathanophas saw three levels of training, where consultants and vendors can first train IT staff, who in turn train individual departmental representatives (sometimes called *superusers*), who finally deliver training to their compatriots within their departments.

The scope of training is demonstrated by the experiences of Pratt and Whitney, Canada (P&WC) in 1998.[4] They trained 110 employees from their six most affected departments as internal trainers (superusers). The year 1998 saw P&WC convert their facilities into a massive class-room, training over 3,000 employees in both technical aspects (system navigation and task training) delivered by consultants as well as providing business-oriented training (processes and tasks). P&WC created over 150 manuals to cover diverse user needs.

Upgrades

Upgrades are mainly intended to take advantage of new technologies and business strategies to ensure that the organization keeps up with the latest business development trends. Therefore, the decision to upgrade SCM and related systems is usually not driven by code deterioration or antici-pated reduction in maintenance costs alone but by different purposes. According to an AMR study, 55% of ERP upgrades were voluntary business improvements triggered by the need for new functionality, expansion, or consolidation of systems; 24% of upgrades were triggered by technology stack changes; 15% of upgrades were forced by discontin-ued support of the running version of software to avoid vendor support termination; and 6% of upgrades were triggered by bug fixes or statutory changes.

The cost of upgrades is high. Upgrade costs may involve 50% of the original software license fee and 20% of the original implementation cost per user, which means over $6 million for a 5,000-user system. Typi-cally, each ERP upgrade requires 8 to 9 months of effort with a team the equivalent of one full-time employee per 35 business users. The adopting organization does not have to develop and rewrite the system itself, but rather it replaces (or upgrades) the old version with a readily available new version from the vendor. However, a lack of experience may cause the costs and length of the upgrade project to approach or even exceed those of the original EIS/ERP implementation effort. General benefits for organizations from EIS/ERP upgrades include the following:

- *Eligibility for help desk support*—Most of software vendors stop providing technical support 12 to 18 months after the next version becomes available. Therefore, keeping up with the pace of vendors will guarantee the support for the system from the vendors.
- *Solutions for outstanding bugs or design weaknesses*—It is impossible to guarantee spotless and error-free systems after the implementations even though vendors will conduct many different testing processes to eliminate the occurrence of errors in the system before the leasing time.
- *New, expanded, or improved features*—Software provides organizations the knowledge and strength (i.e., best practices) from the vendors. Upgrades provide organizations future enhancement from the vendors to give the organizations better opportunities to catch up the current business development, improve their processes and build more efficient business models with new functions, new features and new processing styles provided in the upgraded versions.

Add-ons

Add-on (or bolt-on) is ERP jargon for third-party applications. More specifically, an add-on is an execution system providing very specific functionality or technology to complement ERP software. Many useful applications of this type are available. The types of software and related features of add-on software listed by Microsoft for their ERP software are shown in Table 7.1.

Table 7.1 shows a variety of functions that can still be supported by add-ons. In the 1990s, major functions were supported, such as SCM and CRM. The evolution in ERP systems has seen these major functions pulled into more integrated ERP systems. However, there will always be

Table 7.1. Microsoft ERP Add-ons[5]

Add-on function	Vendor
Automotive ERP	AIM Computer Solutions, Inc.
Distribution, financial, e-commerce integration	Alba Spectrum
Sales and use tax	Avalara
E-commerce	Azox
Automated EDI, XML processing	Data Masons Software
Project tracking, financial	Encore Business Solutions
Electronic invoicing	Enliven Software
Support Excel translation to Dynamics GP	Infinia Business Technology
Payroll and human resources	Integrity Data
Paperless ERP support	Metafile Information Systems
Bar code data capture	Panatrack, Inc.
Document imaging	PaperSavePro
Project resource management	Tenrox
Batch manufacturing support	Vicinity Manufacturing

ideas to supplement ERP systems, some of which will prove commercially viable. A snapshot of some of those systems is demonstrated by Table 7.1.

Support of customer relationship management is the form of data mining most commonly associated with ERP. CRM allows businesses to identify the profitability of specific customers, and to increase chances of retaining them. This is accomplished by having all relevant information readily available that is needed for planning, product, and service throughout the customer life cycle. SAP has been a leader in enhancing their product's abilities to support CRM.[6] Many of these systems failed, as they introduced the need for *middleware*, or software that translates data from one vendor system to another, creating an added layer of complexity and expense.

Naturally, ERP vendors added functionality such as SCM and CRM to more efficiently utilize their systems. As we have mentioned, that is what Oracle did when they purchased Siebel Systems' CRM product in September 2005 and integrated it within their ERP (thus creating an EIS in industry jargon). Thus add-ons became modules through acquisition. Clients benefited by elimination of the need for middleware for that application. However, realistically, there will always be add-on products of some type generated by the active software development industry.

Mortgage Bank Implementation of Enterprise Application Integration

Harmond Bank served the consumer banking market in Ireland. Home loans were among its most profitable business activities. The bank emphasized customer service and sought to lower costs through use of e-business. Much of their mortgage loan process was conducted over the Internet. However, development of diverse systems over time led to many nonintegrated systems. Problems were encountered in efforts to integrate these systems:

- The bank's web portal with online forms for application was based on HTML and Java, running on a Unix-based Apache Web server.
- A back-end mortgage application package ran on Windows NT, obtained from a financial services IT firm.
- A legacy account management system ran on a mainframe using a VME operating system.
- A CRM package ran on Windows NT.
- A Siebel call-center application ran on Windows NT.
- Other software accomplished credit checking, address rating, and other mortgage check.

The lack of integration meant that the bank reentered data across systems, introducing inaccuracies and slowing the loan process. CRM was difficult to implement, because while some systems in the bank had information about specific customers, this information could not be accessed by cross-selling staff.

A team of 12 business and IT professionals was formed within the bank and given 24 months to integrate the banks information systems. Four external consultants were hired to give the team assistance. The first 12 months were dedicated to the home loans divisions. Of this year, 3 months were devoted to BPR, mapping existing mortgage processes and improving them. This led to a plan that would reduce turnaround time in mortgage processing by 50% and would seamlessly integrate and transfer information across bank systems. The plan would be scalable from the current 120 mortgage applications per week to over 300, with acceptable security.

Enterprise application integration (EAI) is a system consisting of middleware to enable communication across applications, adapters to connect these applications to the overall infrastructure, and an integration broker capturing business rules controlling workflow and messaging. EAI significantly reduces the number of interfaces that might be needed, and all components would link to the broker component. Vendors providing EAI tools include IBM, TIBCO, WebMethods, SeeBeyond, and Vitria.

The consultants suggested an EAI for the bank, with a new Siebel-based CRM system more closely coupling CRM with the call center operation. A new plan to install the EIA system in three phases was proposed over a year. Testing led to identification of bugs, extending the project duration 3 months beyond what had been planned. The original 12-month plan was still not completed in 18 months, and project costs exceeded the original budget by 60%. However, the bank's systems were much more efficiently integrated.

The bank considered the effort to have been well-worthwhile, leading to a number of key lessons learned:

- It is best to understand business processes before implementing systems, involving all stakeholders involved.
- Selection of integration architecture is important considering the number of applications to be integrated and the need for real-time data transfer. EAI is not always the appropriate choice.
- EAI packages selected need to have whatever adapters are required for the software to be used within the system. Adapters typically cost around $50,000.
- Some custom coding will be required to link adapters. In the bank's case, the Siebel adapter could be configured using a GUI interface without coding. But the mortgage application package was Java-based, and the adapter needed to be coded, which proved difficult.
- The organizations data structure needed to be analyzed to

avoid duplication and to control updates. System integration solved this, but initially it was a challenge to determine which systems used which data.

- It was found to be more sensible to replace some applications rather than integrating them. The bank's old CRM application was dropped, replaced by a new Siebel call-center application. Using software from as few sources as possible had value.
- EAI requires considerable testing.
- Phased rollout is preferable, controlling the risk of bringing systems online.

Source: Adapted from Lam (2005).

Conclusion

Training is a key component of a successful enterprise system installation. Training needs to be considered in the initial project budget. Typically, it is underestimated by significant amounts. There are two major elements of enterprise system training. The first is focused on how to use the system, and this type of training is well-developed by vendors and consultants. The second is on organization specific business processes. This second form of training has proven to be far more important than the first. Vendors and consultants can't be expected to deliver training programs covering organization-specific processes unless the installed system has no customization. Usually, effective systems that match organizational needs do have customization, and the organization itself will have to develop this form of training. (They will want to if it covers core competencies that yield competitive advantage to the organization.)

An effective means to organize training is to have experts (vendors or consultants) train IT staff. IT staff in turn train a set of superusers from departments within the organization, who then relay the knowledge they obtain to general organizational users.

There are many different media available to deliver enterprise system training. One-way media can be used to inform users of the system's value to the organization. Two-way media are usually more effective in teaching users how to use the system. Hands-on interaction with sandbox systems can be highly effective in training users of their specific job requirements.

Through care in the planning and delivery of training, the success rate of enterprise systems installations can be vastly improved.

EIS/ERP upgrade projects have grown in importance, as vendors are seeking to generate revenue through improved systems. The reticence of vendors to support old systems was noted by multiple organizations in this study. (The value of improved functionality was also noted.)

Upgrade projects seem to be much more controllable than initial supply chain management software installation projects. This should be expected due to the experience organizations gain with their original systems. All the organizations seemed to do something that fit the theoretical model of an upgrade project that we used. Assessment, planning, and action phases were present to at least some degree. The renewal phase noted by the fifteen organizations involved very smooth turnover. A limitation of the study is that future implications were not yet available in all cases (problems may crop up later), although all organizations credited strong planning and project management as ways to assure smooth transitions.

The software industry continues to generate new applications, and improvements on existing applications. That is progress. Large vendors of software will add such systems (or develop their own), leading to the need for upgrades and renewing their revenue stream. Smaller vendors such as Sage and Lawson may not add as many of these functionalities, so that there will be an increasing variety of supply chain software varieties available, calling for more complicated software selection decisions, to include open-source options. The price of progress is often more complexity.

Notes

Chapter 1

1. Ptak and Smith (2011).
2. Manetti (2001).
3. Retrieved July 11, 2011, from http://www.advanced-planning.eu/advanced planninge-356.htm
4. Moser and Ward (2008).
5. Gonzalez (2007).
6. Saenz de Ugarte et al. (2009).
7. Olson and Kesharwani (2010).
8. Olson (2004).
9. Mabert et al. (2000); Olhager and Selldin (2003); Katerattanakul et al. (2006).

Chapter 2

1. Fishman (2006).
2. Holzner (2006).
3. Brady et al. (2001).
4. Mabert et al. (2000); Olhager and Selldin (2003).
5. Stevens (2001).
6. Davenport (1998).
7. Davenport (1998).
8. Stadtler (2005)
9. Wiers (2009).

Chapter 3

1. Schwartz (2003).
2. "Outsourcing's next generation" (2003).

Chapter 4

1. Hall et al. (1993).
2. Scott and Kaindle (2000).
3. Hammer and Stanton (1999).

Chapter 5

1. Kwahk and Ahn (2010).
2. See Aberdeen Group annual reports, available at http://www.aberdeen .com/Research/Research.aspx.
3. Keen (1988).
4. Olson (1996).
5. Edwards (1977).
6. See Gartner Group or Standish Group reports of industry project performance on an annual basis.
7. Perera and Costa (2008).
8. Olson (2011).

Chapter 6

1. Mabert et al. (2000); Olhager and Selldin (2003).
2. Schonberger (1981).
3. Goldratt (1997).
4. Goldratt (1997).

Chapter 7

1. Ngai and Law (2008).
2. Tsai and Hung (2008).
3. Vathanophas (2007).
4. Swanton (2004).
5. ERP Software blog, retrieved July 28, 2011, from http://www.erpsoftware blog.com/members/partners-add-on/
6. Olson and Shi (2006).

References

Brady, J. A., Monk, E. F., & Wagner, B. J. (2001). *Concepts in enterprise resource planning*. Boston, MA: Course Technology.

Bryson, K. M., & Sullivan, W. E. (2003). Designing effective incentive-oriented contracts for application service provider hosting of ERP systems. *Business Process Management Journal, 9*(6), 705–721.

Clymer, J. (2004, October 9). Rent or buy? *PC Magazine, 23*(18), pp. 129–132, 136, 138.

Dai, Z. (2008). Supply chain transformation by ERP for enhancing performance: An empirical investigation. *Advances in Competitiveness Research, 16*(1), 87–98.

Davenport, T. H. (1998, July–August). Putting the enterprise into the enterprise system. *Harvard Business Review, 76*(4), 121–131.

Dhillon, G., & Caldeira, M. (2008). A bumpy road to success (or not): The case of Project Genesis at Nevada DMV. *International Journal of Information Management, 28*, 222–228.

Edwards, W. E. (1977). How to use multiattribute utility measurement for social decisionmaking. *IEEE Transactions on Systems, Man, and Cybernetics SMC, 7*(5), 326–340.

ERP outsourcing. (2003, June). *CIO Insight, 27*, 72.

Fishman, C. (2006). *The Walmart effect: How the world's most powerful company really works—and how it's transforming the American economy*. New York, NY: Penguin Books.

Goldratt, E. M. (1997). *Critical chain*. Great Barrington, MA: The North River Press.

Gonzalez, A. (2007). Surveying the TMS landscape. *Supply Chain Management Review, 11*(1), 36–40.

Hall, G., Rosenthal, J., & Wade, J. (1993). How to make reengineering work. *Harvard Business Review, 71*(6), 119–131.

Hammer, M., & Stanton, S. (1999). How process enterprises really work. *Harvard Business Review, 77*(10), 108–118.

Holzner, S. (2006). *How Dell does it: Using speed and innovation to achieve extraordinary results*. New York, NY: McGraw-Hill.

Katerattanakul, P., Hong, S., & Lee, J. (2006). Enterprise resource planning survey of Korean manufacturing firms. *Management Research News, 29*(12), 820–837.

Keen, P. G. W. (1988). Value analysis: Justifying decision support systems. *MIS Quarterly, 5*(1), 1–16.

Kwahk, K.-Y., & Ahn, H. (2010). Moderating effects of localization differences on ERP use: A socio-technical systems perspective. *Computers in Human Behavior, 26,* 186–198.

Lam, W. (2005). An enterprise application integration (EAI) case-study: Seamless mortgage processing at Harmond Bank. *Journal of Computer Information Systems, 46*(1), 35–43.

Mabert, V. M., Soni, A., & Venkataramanan, M. A. (2000). Enterprise resource planning survey of manufacturing firms. *Production and Inventory Management Journal, 41*(20), 52–58.

Manetti, J. (2001). How technology is transforming manufacturing. *Production and Inventory Management Journal, 42*(1), 54–64.

McCubbrey, D. J., & Fukami, C. V. (2009). ERP at the Colorado Department of Transportation: The whistle blower's dilemma. *Communications of the Association for Information Systems, 24*(7), 105–112.

Moser, G., & Ward, P. (2008). Which TMS is right for you? *Supply Chain Management Review, 12*(3), 50–56.

Ngai, E. W. T., & Law, C. C. H. (2008). Examining the critical success factors in the adoption of enterprise resource planning systems. *Computers in Industry, 59*(6), 548–564.

Olhager, J., & Selldin, E. (2003). Enterprise resource planning survey of Swedish manufacturing firms. *European Journal of Operational Research, 146*(2), 365–373.

Olson, D. L. (1996). *Decision aids for selection problems.* New York, NY: Springer.

Olson, D. L. (2004). *Managerial issues of enterprise resource planning systems.* Boston, MA: McGraw-Hill/Irwin.

Olson, D. L. (2011). *Supply chain risk management.* New York, NY: Business Expert Press.

Olson, D. L., & Kesharwani, S. (2010). *Enterprise information systems: Contemporary trends and issues.* Hackensack, NJ: World Scientific.

Olson, D. L., & Shi, Y. (2006). *Introduction to business data mining.* New York, NY: McGraw-Hill/Irwin.

Olson, D. L., & Staley, J. (2012). Case study of open-source enterprise resource planning implementation in a small business. *Enterprise Information Systems* (in press).

Outsourcing's next generation. (June 23, 2003). *Eweek, 20*(25), 22–24.

Perera, H. S. C., & Costa, W. K. R. (2008). Analytic hierarchy process for selection of ERP software for manufacturing companies. *The Journal of Business Perspective, 12*(4), 1–11.

Ptak, C., & Smith, C. (2011). *Orlicky's Material Requirements Planning* (3rd ed.). New York, NY: McGraw-Hill Professional.

Rudberg, M., & Thulin, J. (2009). Centralised supply chain master planning employing advanced planning systems. *Production Planning & Control*, *20*(2), 158–167.

Saenz de Ugarte, B., Artiba, A., & Pellerin, R. (2009). Manufacturing execution system—A literature review. *Production Planning & Control*, *20*(6), 525–539.

Schonberger, R. J. (1981). Why projects are "always" late: A rationale based on manual simulation of a PERT/CPM network. *Interfaces*, *11*(5), 66–70.

Schwartz, J. A. (2003, November 10). A clean, fresh feeling. *VarBusiness*, *19*(23), pp. 24–26, 28, 30.

Scott, E., & Kaindle, L. (2000). Enhancing functionality in an enterprise software package. *Information & Management*, *37*(2), 111–122.

Stadtler, H. (2005). Supply chain management and advanced planning—Basics, overview and challenges. *European Journal of Operational Research*, *163*(3), 575–588.

Stevens, T. (2001, April 16). All's fair in integration. *Industry Week*, pp. 24–29.

Swanton, B. (2004, September 21). Build ERP upgrade costs into the business change program—not the IT budget. *Computer Weekly*, p. 28.

Tsai, W.-H., & Hung, S.-J. (2008). E-commerce implementation: An empirical study of the performance of enterprise resource planning systems using the organizational learning model. *International Journal of Management*, *25*(2), 348–352.

Vathanophas, V. (2007). Business process approach toward an inter-organizational enterprise system. *Business Process Management Journal*, *13*(3), 433–450.

Wiers, V. C. S. (2009). The relationship between shop floor autonomy and APS implementation success: Evidence from two cases. *Production Planning and Control*, *20*(7), 576–585.

Index

software systems
  selection criteria, 102
  for supply chain management,
    41–54
  upgrades, 106–107
Standish Group surveys, 86
strategic planning, enterprise requirements planning software,
  14–15
superusers
  software training for, 106
  training for, 111
supply chain information systems
  add-ons, 107–108
  basic properties, 1
  critical path models, 94–102
  enterprise requirements planning
    systems, 11–17
  execution applications, 4
  historical evolution of, 4–5
  online marketplaces, 17–19
  open-source software, 46–47
  outsourcing of, 45–46
  planning applications, 4
  product, information, and financial
    streams, 4
  selection criteria, 65–83
  software components, 4, 81–83
  upgrades, 106–107
supply chain management (SCM)
  enterprise requirements planning
    systems, 15–17
  historical evolution, 1–2
  installation project management,
    85–102
  software source comparisons,
    47–48
  software systems, 11, 41–54
  system selection criteria, 65–83
  training issues in, 103–106
  value analysis in, 72–76
supply chain processes, 2–3

T
Taylor, Frederick, 55
technology-enabled reengineering,
  supply chain management using,
  60–62

third-party software, ERP system variants, 27–28
time horizons, cost-benefit analysis,
  67–68
Tiny ERP, 46–47
total cost of ownership (TCO), supply chain management software
  systems, 65–66
training for software use
  costs of, 66
  critical importance of, 103–106, 111
  enterprise requirements planning
    systems, 13–17
  installation project management
    and costs of, 88
  media tools for, 105–106, 111–112
  problems, 104–105
transportation management systems
  (TMSs) software, 9–10

U
uncertainty, advanced planning systems and, 38–40
up-front expenditures, cost-benefit
  analysis, supply chain software, 68
upgrades, 112
  supply chain information systems,
    106–107

V
value analysis, cost-benefit analysis
  and, 72–76, 83
value score, in simple multiattribute
  rating technique, 80
Vathanophas, V., 106
vehicle assembly case study, materials
  requirements planning, 28–37
vendor advantage
  ERP system variants, 27–28
  in value analysis, 74–76
vendor-based software modules
  business process reengineering, 59–60
  case study using, 50–54
  installation project management
    and costs, 88
  supply chain management
    software, 43
Visual ERP software, 51–54

Announcing the Business Expert Press Digital Library

Concise E-books Business Students
Need for Classroom and Research

This book can also be purchased in an e-book collection by your library as

- a one-time purchase,
- that is owned forever,
- allows for simultaneous readers,
- has no restrictions on printing,
- can be downloaded as PDFs from within the library community.

Our digital library collections are a great solution to beat the rising cost of textbooks. E-books can be loaded into their course management systems or onto students' e-book readers.

The **Business Expert Press** digital libraries are very affordable, with no obligation to buy in future years.

For more information, please visit **www.businessexpertpress.com/librarians**. To set up a trial in the United States, please contact **Sheri Dean** at sheri.dean@globalepress.com; for all other regions, contact **Nicole Lee** at *nicole.lee@igroupnet.com*.

OTHER TITLES IN OUR SUPPLY AND OPERATIONS MANAGEMENT COLLECTION

Series Editor: **Steven Nahmias,** *Santa Clara University*

- *Production Line Efficiency: A Comprehensive Guide for Managers* by Sabry Shaaban and Sarah Hudson
- *Transforming US Army Supply Chains: Strategies for Management Innovation* by Greg Parlier
- *Design, Analysis and Optimization of Supply Chains: A System Dynamics Approach* by William R. Killingsworth
- *Supply Chain Planning and Analytics: The Right Product in the Right Place at the Right Time* by Gerald Feigin
- *Supply-Chain Survival in the Age of Globalization* by James A. Pope
- *Better Business Decisions Using Cost Modeling: For Procurement, Operations, and Supply Chain Professionals* by Victor E. Sower and Christopher Sower

CPSIA information can be obtained at www.ICGtesting.com
Printed in the USA
BVOW010239120412

287396BV00004B/5/P

9 781606 493601